THE COMPLETE GUIDE TO

REMODELING
YOUR BASEMENT

THE COMPLETE GUIDE TO

REMODELING YOUR BASEMENT

How to Create New Living Space the Professional Way

GARY D. BRANSON

BETTERWAY PUBLICATIONS, INC.
WHITE HALL, VIRGINIA

Published by Betterway Publications, Inc.
Box 219
Crozet, VA 22932
(804) 823-5661

Cover by Susan Riley
Cover photography courtesy of the Plywood Paneling Council
Text photographs (in order of appearance): United Gilsonite Laboratories
(UGL products), The Bilco Co. (basement doors) 203-934-6363, Plywood
Paneling Council, City of Richfield, MN (permits), Sears, Clairson Inter-
national (Closet Maid) 1-800-874-0008, Sico Inc. (Room Makers) 1-800-
328-6138, United States Gypsum (USG products), Owens/Corning Fiber-
glas, Heat-N-Glo Fireplace Products Inc. 612-890-8367, Gold Bond Build-
ing Products, Decorate It! 1-800-828-3300, Armstrong World Industries,
Inc.
Typography by East Coast Typography, Inc.

Library of Congress Cataloging-in-Publication Data

Branson, Gary D.
  The complete guide to remodeling your basement : how to create new
living space the professional way / by Gary D. Branson.
      p.   cm.
  Includes index.
  ISBN: 1-55870-162-1 : $14.95
  1. Basements — Remodeling.   I. Title
TH4816.3.B35B73   1990
643'.5 — dc20   90-39100
                                                                      CIP

Printed in the United States of America
0 9 8 7 6 5 4 3 2

Dedicated to
my father
Hugh J. Branson
Who taught me the trades

Acknowledgments

Our thanks to:

Betterway Staff
People . . .

Contents

Introduction

I am a contributing editor to *Workbench* magazine. In the October '89 issue I wrote an article that was titled "Basement Remodeling." The article was produced from materials that had been developed for a series of television shows for "Hometime." Shortly after the article appeared I received a query from Mr. Robert Hostage of Betterway Publications, Inc. Would I be interested in expanding the magazine article into a book about basement remodeling? We both agreed that, considering the number of houses built with basement space roughed in, ready for future finishing, a book on the subject might be useful. Thus began *The Complete Guide to Remodeling Your Basement*.

I began my construction career in Wichita, Kansas. To keep me busy during summer school vacation my father put me to work on his construction crew at the age of thirteen. By age twenty I had my own subcontracting business. Over the years I have held union membership in both the plasterer's and painter's unions. I was a drywall (wallboard) contractor and installed, finished and spray textured wallboard in more than 1,000 new homes, over a period of twenty-five years.

In 1955 I moved from Wichita, where a building boom was ending, to Minneapolis, Minnesota, where building was brisk. In Minneapolis I had my own construction business for twenty-two years. I subcontracted in new construction, but Minnesota winters can be cold, and construction activities such as pouring concrete and applying plaster or paint tend to lag in the winter. When cold weather came I kept busy by doing remodeling work. The Twin Cities area had thousands of "expansion-type" houses that were built with attics large enough to be finished for living space as young families grew. We finished hundreds of these attic expansions, as well as converting many basements to living space. During the period I encountered just about every possible construction problem.

I solicited the remodeling work through advertisements placed in the newspaper. From the telephone number in the ads, people were able to contact me for free advice. Some callers pretended they wanted to hire me, though in fact they were "picking my brain" for any free information they could get. Some readily admitted they intended to do the work themselves, but needed expert advice. Would I help? I never refused to help anyone who asked, and I never regretted giving the help. I felt I learned as much as I taught.

In time, after answering hundreds of calls, I believed that there might be a market for written how-to advice. I wrote an article and sold it to a magazine. From that beginning I wrote many magazine articles, then a book, on various how-to subjects. In 1977 I accepted a job as an editor for a home repair magazine called *The Family Handyman.*

My contractor's experience in advice-by-phone proved valuable. I began to do promotional media work for the magazine. Eventually this effort expanded to doing talk radio and TV in 22 cities, coast to coast. I began my talk radio experience at WOR in New York City.

I also took phone queries from readers of the magazine, and did a column that answered readers' queries. I talked to thousands of people, and I believe I've gained a fairly accurate understanding of the kinds of advice the homeowner needs. I hope some of that experience is reflected in these pages, and that you find something of value here.

This book, as the title suggests, was written primarily for the person who wants to finish his/her basement. But I also hope the book will be useful reading for those who are adding onto the house, or who are finishing an attic expansion, or who are contracting their own new house. The information should be applicable to any one who owns a home.

I hope, too, that this book will serve as a sort of "consumer protection" guide. One deplorable scam is the use of false or irrelevant claims for the building materials you buy. I refer to the bandwagon effect such as was seen during the height of the energy crisis. Manufacturers of all sorts of materials were attributing high R-values to their products, to take advantage of consumers' concerns about energy costs and supplies. Do Brand "X" roof shingles have a high R-factor? That may be true, but it is irrelevant, because the R-factor of your roof shingles has *no* bearing — *none at all* — on your heating bill. No product beyond the insulation barrier in your attic can possibly conserve heat for your house.

And I deplore the number of homeowners who are bilked out of their money in phony basement waterproofing schemes costing thousands of dollars per house. Ninety-five percent or more of all wet basement problems can be cured by finding the path that rain follows into your basement and — inexpensively — blocking that path. See the Water Problems section of Chapter 1 for advice. And, for advice on hiring a contractor, see Chapter 13, HOW TO HIRE A CONTRACTOR.

1
Should You Finish Your Basement?

Perhaps your basement is under a modern house, with plumbing roughed in and room dimensions defined: a basement that was built with the intent that it would one day become part of the living space. On the other hand, suppose your basement is little more than a cellar and contains an old-fashioned "octopus" furnace, a coal chute, and racks to hold screens or storm windows depending on the season. Should you finish your basement? If you need extra living space, even the cellar can become attractive and usable space.

One example I recall was a 90-year-old farm house with a cellar roughly 20 feet square, or about 400 sq. ft. of usable floorspace. The owner had three teen-age children and decided to finish the basement as a rec room to take the wear and tear away from her living room. The contractor was most doubtful of the possibilities when he observed the crumbling sandstone walls, the cracked floor, and the low headroom. But the lady had her own plans for the space: all she wanted was someone to carry out her plan. The sandstone walls were plastered with a stucco-like finish; pipes were moved to make a clean surface for application of a wall-board ceiling; and a large hole was cut into the reinforced floor of her living room. A circular stair was installed in the hole and the former cellar be-

came a very attractive extension of the living room above; an extension that isolated noise and provided privacy while being in reality only an 8-foot deep "conversation pit."

While recalling worst-case examples, it is true that some basements simply are not very good candidates for finishing. Make an inventory of the problems in your basement and decide whether they can be corrected before making any decision to invest your time and money.

THE SPACE: HOW USABLE?

The first step is to decide what you will use the space for. Is there sufficient headroom? Comfort requires, and building codes may decree, that your basement have a minimum of 7½ feet of headroom. Many houses, especially those tract houses built right after World War II, were built with ten-course basements. This means that the concrete blocks were stacked only ten courses (rows) high, yielding only a scant 7 feet of headspace (ten rows of 8″ block, plus mortar joints).

Consider also that steel or wooden support beams which run down the center of the floor can be enclosed or otherwise dealt with. But in older houses, where attempts have been made to reinforce sagging floors, one may find support beams and posts that must either be relocated at some expense and effort, or will so obstruct any rational planning as to make the job inadvisable.

Converted furnaces with huge "octopus" ducts may also provide a barrier to a successful basement remodel. If the old furnace is due for replacement and you are prepared to pay the cost of a complete overhaul of the system, finishing the basement may then be worthwhile. Stairway location too can be a problem, but it is not terribly difficult to reposition the stairway if that is the only objection to the project (see PLANNING AND JOB SEQUENCE, Chapter 2).

ACCESSIBILITY

Does your basement have windows large enough to provide light and ventilation? Without such windows a basement can be a dungeon. Does the basement have an exterior door, or are windows large enough so that an adult person can crawl through them to escape a fire or other emergency? Your building code may require optional basement exits for basement space that is occupied (see PLANNING AND JOB SEQUENCE, Chapter 2).

BASEMENT WATER AND MOISTURE

Moisture Problems

A common sight for contractors or building inspectors is to find basement windows that have not been opened for many years. Often, one will see basement windows that obviously have been painted shut. This is always the case when one finds strong mildew or mold odors, black mildew stains on walls or undersides of floors, or water stains at low levels on concrete walls, where the walls meet the concrete floors. Owners or occupants often complain of the odors when quite obviously they could be eliminated by opening the windows, perhaps using fans to pull the fresh outdoor air in an open basement window at one end of the basement and out through another open window at the opposite end. Fresh air, which can contain little humidity on a warm summer day, will not only pick up excess basement moisture and remove it, the air will freshen the interior as nothing else will.

Basement surfaces such as concrete floors and walls are usually cooler than the air, so any moisture will condense when it reaches the cool concrete, and form droplets of moisture. This appearance of moisture forming on cold surfaces is a sure sign that humidity is building up in the basement, and that additional air circulation or ventilation is needed. Not only will the accumulated moisture damage the building materials in the basement, the high humidity is very uncomfortable for the occupants of the space.

Open the windows, and consider installing vents in areas where moisture is present. No pro is impressed with those vent dampers that let the dryer exhaust spent heat and moisture into living space. The heat thus saved is negligible: one obviously should not use such a device on gas clothes dryers or other appliances, and the potential for creating moisture problems in the house is very high. Vent dryers directly outdoors to get rid of the moisture: the reclaimed heat from 3 or 4 loads of dried clothes per week is negligible.

Be aware of the potential for moisture problems when you choose the materials for finishing your basement. For example, use louvered doors instead of solid slab doors, so moisture will not be trapped in closets or laundry space. Choose open shelves and wire baskets for storing clothes, rather than closed drawers that will trap moisture. Any basement bathroom should have an exhaust fan, preferably connected to the light so the exhaust is running anytime the light is on.

Basement Water

Few problems have provided a greater opportunity for homeowner rip-offs than wet basements. And yet, the National Association of Home Builders has always maintained that the great majority of wet basements are wet because roof and ground water are permitted to run into the basement. The NAHB estimates that perhaps 95% of all wet basements could be dried up inexpensively, usually by the homeowner's own efforts.

Basement waterproofing contractors maintain that the cause of the wet basement is a "high water table." The water table is the depth at which the ground or soil is totally saturated with water. A call to your local building inspector, or a local excavating contractor, will inform you where the water table is in your area. Keep in mind that modern building departments seek to avoid problems with new houses, and will not issue building permits for basements if they believe that the water table will cause the homeowner future trouble. Another potential problem is for the building department or city itself: permitting construction in areas where the water table is high causes the city problems with the sewer system, because any water that enters the basement ultimately winds up going down the floor drain and into the sewer treatment facility.

For further convincing, consider this quote from HouseMaster of America, a national network of home inspectors: "Based on HouseMaster of America's experience, most wet basement conditions could be alleviated with minimum effort and expense. This is due to the fact that most water penetration (into basements) occurs because its major causes — rain water from the roof and surface water — are not attended to, and water accumulates around the perimeter of the house and eventually seeps in." The key here is the phrase "alleviated with minimum effort and expense." This means that you may have problems with roof rain gutters, or with the grade of the lawn around

your basement. If the grade (slope) of your lawn is such that it lets water run back toward the basement, the water will find its way into the basement. Use a level and straight 2 × 4 to check the slope of the lawn on all sides of your basement.

Be aware that digging a flower bed or installing a concrete slab for a walk, drive, or patio may disturb the grade that was established by the builder, and you must add dirt to reestablish a good slope on all sides of the basement. Be aware, too, that the presence or absence of roof rain gutters on your house is not significant. If you have no rain gutters it simply means that the contractor checked that particular site for grade or slope, the width of the roof overhang, and the proximity of your house to your neighbor's house. The builder then decided that the basement would stay dry without having rain gutters: he may have made a bad decision, and some future development shows that rain gutters are needed to collect the rain water and snow melt from your roof and deposit it far away from the foundation or basement walls. Many people will stubbornly assert that the house doesn't need rain gutters, simply because it has never had gutters: never mind that there has been a long-term water problem with the basement.

If you have gutters and you still have basement water problems, check the condition of the gutters. Gutters that are loose, or sagging, or rusted through can collect vast amounts of water and then deliver it all in one spot, where it can seep back against the basement wall and enter there. Repair, replace, or reattach gutters as needed. Check also to see if the ground pipes are in place and are delivering water at least 6 to 8 feet away from the basement wall. If you observe houses as you drive through your city you will note that many have downspouts that dump roof water in a pool next to the basement wall: there are no ground pipes at the bottom to carry the water away. If you look in the bushes, you may see that the problem is simply a missing ground pipe: the person who mows the lawn just throws the ground

White powder or stains at corners be-tween walls or walls and floor indicate efflorescence from moisture problems. Photo courtesy of United Gilsonite Laboratories.

To check moisture source, tape aluminum foil on the concrete wall. Check after 24–48 hours. Moisture on back of foil indi-cates seepage or leaks; moisture on foil face indicates condensation (high humid-ity). Basement may have either, or both, problems. Photo courtesy of United Gilsonite Laboratories.

Mix etching chemical into water as directed on label instructions. Etching product etches and cleans the concrete surface. Note rubber gloves; also wear eye goggles for protection. Photo courtesy of United Gilsonite Laboratories.

Use nylon brush to apply the etching chemical to the efflorescence. A 5% solution of muriatic acid can also be used for cleaning concrete. Photo courtesy of United Gilsonite Laboratories.

Use a wire brush and scraper to clean away slag and efflorescence. Wear eye goggles. Photo courtesy of United Gilsonite Laboratories.

Fill minor holes and level form marks in concrete with Portland cement or patching product. Photo courtesy of United Gilsonite Laboratories.

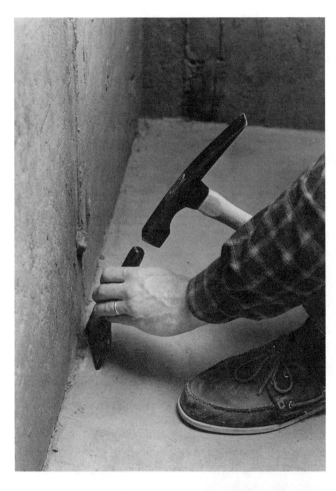

Cracks between floor and walls should be filled with hydraulic (waterproof) cement. Widen crack with a mason's chisel and hammer. Widening the crack permits penetration of hydraulic patching into crack. Photo courtesy of United Gilsonite Laboratories.

Use a mason's pointing trowel to apply hydraulic cement patching to the floor cracks. Note worker is applying patching material at 45-degree angle up the wall. Photo courtesy of United Gilsonite Laboratories.

Use a nylon brush to apply a quality masonry waterproofer to all walls, as a final insurance against future leakage. Photo courtesy of United Gilsonite Laboratories.

pipe in the bushes to avoid having to move it each time he mows. Each downspout can easily deposit 200 to 300 gallons of water against the basement wall: a 1 inch rain deposits 1,200 gallons of water on a 1,200 sq. ft. roof. Replace or add ground pipes.

If leaks persist take a walk around the house during a heavy rain, and try to see the flow patterns the water makes. You may spot a steady stream of water that runs directly toward a wall or window well. Your task then will be to provide a diversion so the water will run away, rather than toward, the house. Solving your water problem may be as simple as installing a plastic cover over a window well, or damming the water's path with a wheelbarrow of dirt.

Finally, seal all cracks in the basement with patching (hydraulic) cement. Then apply one or more coats of waterproofing sealer to the interior side of the walls, to seal out water, insects, and radon.

DRAIN MAINTENANCE

In the past, homeowners have considered that the proper time to clean sewer drains is after they have backed up into the basement and caused a mess. A much wiser approach is to consider drain cleaning to be a regular maintenance procedure rather than an emergency, after-the-fact job. It is only good sense to clean drains periodically to avoid the damage and inconvenience of water in the basement.

In most metropolitan areas cleaning the main sewer drain (from the house to the street sewer main) involves having a professional run a steel cable device through the 4-inch diameter drain pipe. At the end of the steel cable is a set of revolving steel blades that scrape the interior of the pipe free of grease, hair, tree roots, and other obstructions. Because city lots usually have short setbacks (the distance from the front of houses to the curb or street) of under 50 feet, figure a charge of

$100 to be at least a starting point for estimating the cost of sewer drain cleaning. The charge obviously may vary widely, governed by such factors as the general economy in your area, whether servicemen are paid union wages, the length of the sewer drain pipe, and whether the pipe is already partially clogged with tree roots, which may take hours to cut through. The best approach is to look for special rates offered by plumbers or sewer cleaning services during winter or off-season times when a non-emergency, routine cleaning can often be had at near half-price rates.

Ask the serviceman how often you should have your sewer drains cleaned. If you have problems with tree roots penetrating into sewer pipes and clogging them, the serviceman may suggest an annual cleaning; if there are no trees to block sewer drains, you might be safe in having the drains cleaned every two years.

Whatever your serviceman suggests, it is wise to follow his advice and observe preventive maintenance with drains. Neglected drains can fill with roots until the cast iron drain pipe breaks. Then, your only option is to have the drain pipes excavated and replaced. Even the cost of sewer drain replacement may be minor, compared to the mess and damage to walls, furniture, and carpets from a backed-up sewer drain.

ASBESTOS

Asbestos is a known cause of such diseases as lung cancer, asbestosis, and mesothelioma. The evidence is that asbestos-related diseases are most common in industrial workers who have been exposed to asbestos over a period of years. Even with daily exposure, it takes years for asbestos-related diseases to reveal themselves. There is no recognized safe exposure level for asbestos.

As long as asbestos is not disturbed so that fibers can become airborne, it does not pose a health hazard. If you are remodeling, leave any asbestos products in place if possible. For example, you might just place another layer of plywood over floorcovering that contains asbestos, rather than removing it.

If you remove old ceiling tile in a basement remodeling, or if you decide to replace old heating equipment that has asbestos insulation covering pipes or ducts, you may wish to contact your local Environmental Protection Agency office for advice. The EPA offers a homeowners' guide titled *Asbestos in the Home*. The EPA also has a list of approved Asbestos Abatement Removal Contractors. Don't fall for any hustlers who are cashing in on asbestos fears.

RADON

Radon is a radioactive gas that is odorless, colorless, and tasteless, and is generally thought to be second only to smoking as a cause of lung cancer. Radon became an issue when it was found in high levels in houses that were built with materials that had been contaminated by uranium mine waste, back in the '60s.

How serious is the risk? The Environmental Protection Agency suspects that radon may be responsible for as many as 100 lung cancer deaths per day. It is believed that the risk increases with exposure. Most risk estimates are based on lifetime or long-term exposure, plus the level of radon contamination.

Radon is measured in picocuries. A picocurie is 1/trillionth of a curie, a unit of measure for radioactivity. The permissible limit for radon is set at 4 picocuries per liter of air, shown as 4 pCi/l.

To assess the risk, consider that one source estimates your lung cancer risk from 4pCi/l to be equal to the risk of dying in a home accident: the risk at 20 pCi/l radon exposure is equal to the risk of dying from an auto accident. But the jury is still out: recent reports indicate that the state of Iowa may have the highest concentration of radon in the nation, but Iowa has a low rate of lung cancer. What is certain is that radon is definitely suspect; that radon levels are greatest in the basement, and anyone who contemplates finishing off basement space would be prudent to do some preliminary testing for radon.

It is obvious that one factor is the way we live and use our houses. Those who spend a great deal of time in a basement workshop, or who have bedrooms or recreation rooms in the basement are at greater risk than those who spend little time at home.

There are areas where radon levels are known to be high, but radon should generally be monitored on a house-by-house basis, because radon can appear anywhere. And, despite the media attention given to radon, statistics indicate that the majority of homeowners have not tested their homes for radon. If you plan to finish off your basement — or even if you don't — you should test for radon.

Home centers and department stores offer radon test canisters containing activated charcoal. Just open the canister and leave the unit in the basement for 3 to 7 days. Then close and seal the canister and send it off to a laboratory. The cost for this test, including postage and laboratory work, can be about $20. Another test device is called an alpha track unit. The test uses a sheet of polycarbonate plastic as a recording surface. The exposed plastic sheet is struck by alpha particles from decaying radon, and is left in place for 3 to 6 months. Then the dents in the plastic are counted by a laboratory to find the level of radon present. This test costs between $25 and $50. If these low-cost tests show no radon, or show levels under the 4 pCi/1 permissible level, it is safe to proceed. In most cases the level of radon will not increase, but you may decide to retest from time to time to be sure radon levels are safe.

If tests show higher levels of radon, do not panic and let yourself be the victim of any radon control rip-offs. One home in an area known for high radon levels, the "Reading Prong" in New Jersey, showed radon levels at 3500 pCi/1: a contractor reduced this level to 2 pCi/1 in one day's work, for a total cost of $1,300. If radon levels are high, contact your state radiation protection office for further advice.

Remember that the repairs recommended for radon control are good basic procedures to control air infiltration and moisture and insect entry as well. Caulk or patch (with hydraulic cement, if there is also a threat of water seepage) any cracks in basement walls or floor. Then apply a coat of waterproofing sealer such as United Gilsonite Laboratories' (UGL) Drylok to all walls. Install ducts so that furnaces, fireplaces, or dryers can draw outside air for combustion or for drying. Appliances that draw combustion air from the interior will create low indoor air pressure and increase radon infiltration.

Provide ventilation so that fresh air continually flows into and out of the basement. There is almost no health threat that is not decreased by good ventilation: radon, moisture/humidity and chemicals such as formaldehyde all are reduced or eliminated by continuous ventilation of the basement or workplace.

Some states or local governments offer free radon detectors: your local building inspector should be able to help you locate the right office for radiation protection. Or, call your regional Environmental Protection Agency office, as shown on the next page.

EFFECT ON RESALE VALUE

A common subject for discussion on homes has been the effect of certain remodeling projects on resale value. Finishing a basement can return the project's cost — or more, depending on whether you do it yourself or pay contractor prices — if the basement is a walkout or daylight basement. Walkout or daylight simply means that the base-

STATE — EPA REGION

Alabama — 4	Kentucky — 4	North Dakota — 8
Alaska — 10	Louisiana — 6	Ohio — 5
Arizona — 9	Maine — 1	Oklahoma — 6
Arkansas — 6	Maryland — 3	Oregon — 10
California — 9	Massachusetts — 1	Pennsylvania — 3
Colorado — 8	Michigan — 5	Rhode Island — 1
Connecticut — 1	Minnesota — 5	South Carolina — 4
Delaware — 3	Mississippi — 4	South Dakota — 8
District of Columbia — 3	Missouri — 7	Tennessee — 4
Florida — 4	Montana — 8	Texas — 6
Georgia — 4	Nebraska — 7	Utah — 8
Hawaii — 9	Nevada — 9	Vermont — 1
Idaho — 10	New Hampshire — 1	Virginia — 3
Illinois — 5	New Jersey — 2	Washington — 10
Indiana — 5	New Mexico — 6	West Virginia — 3
Iowa — 7	New York — 2	Wisconsin — 5
Kansas — 7	North Carolina — 4	Wyoming — 8

EPA REGIONAL OFFICES

EPA Region 1
Room 2203
JFK Federal Building
Boston, MA 02203
(617) 223-4845

EPA Region 2
26 Federal Plaza
New York, NY 10278
(212) 264-2515

EPA Region 3
841 Chestnut Street
Philadelphia, PA 19107
(215) 597-8320

EPA Region 5
230 South Dearborn Street
Chicago, IL 60604
(312) 353-2205

EPA Region 6
1445 Ross Avenue
Dallas, TX 75202-2733
(214) 655-7208

EPA Region 7
726 Minnesota Avenue
Kansas City, KS 66101
(913) 236-2803

EPA Region 4
345 Courtland Street, NE
Atlanta, GA 30365
(404) 881-3776

EPA Region 8
Suite 1300
One Denver Place
999 18th Street
Denver, CO 80202
(303) 283-1710

EPA Region 9
215 Fremont Street
San Francisco, CA 94105
(415) 974-8076

EPA Region 10
1200 Sixth Avenue
Seattle, WA 98101
(206) 442-7660

ment level is partially exposed, so that doors and windows open onto ground level or grade. If the basement space is below grade so that no ground level entry door is possible, and windows are high and small so they let in little sunlight, any return on remodeling investment will be limited.

If you do most of the remodeling work yourself, so the cash investment is for materials only, you should get back a marginal return. If you pay contractor's prices, you will be fortunate to get back 100% of your investment. Many texts treat a 100% return on remodeling investment as though that return was a worthwhile goal. But, getting back 100% simply means that you have traded dollars: you have not made a profit. There is no profit in sticking $6,000 into a project, simply in the hope of getting it back out. You are better off to leave the money in a bank than undertake the remodeling.

Let's illustrate the point: Two divorced women lived in houses exactly alike and side by side. Both had divorce agreements with ex-husbands that they would occupy their houses until minor children graduated high school; each house would then be sold and the proceeds split between the woman and her ex-husband.

Both put their houses up for sale at the same time in the summer of '89. One woman listed her house for $74,900. She did no work on the house to ready it for sale, nor to try to increase the sale price. The neighbor called in a contractor and finished off the basement at a cost of over $6,000. By doing this she hoped to increase her final profit, and listed for $84,900. The results? Both houses were slow to sell. But the one with the unfinished basement sold in about 90 days,

for $73,000. The house with the finished basement and the higher price sat unsold for months. Finally, the house was sold for $78,000, or only $5,000 more than the house with the unfinished basement.

What was the effect of finishing the basement and setting the higher price? First, the seller increased the asking price so the house was offered at the top of the scale for houses in that area. Next, she forced the buyer to come up with a slightly higher down payment, and the house would have slightly higher monthly payments. Also, she increased the agent's fee by $700 — if she had gotten her asking price, it would have increased by 7% × 10,000 or $700.

Not only did the woman who remodeled not get back a profit for her investment, she actually may have made the house less desirable than if she had left the space unfinished. Many young couples, looking at unfinished space in a basement or attic, see the space as an opportunity to save money by doing the work themselves. And, if they don't need the space, they will see the higher price as a barrier to buying the house.

There are no rules in real estate. If you're a smart buyer, and a good planner, you may succeed where others would fail. The best advice, however, is to finish basement (or attic) space only when you need the space for your own family, and only when you intend to stay and use that space for a period of at least several years. The use of the space constitutes a return on your investment, and a well-executed basement remodeling should yield back at least as much as it cost — or more, if you do a good job of planning and executing your remodel.

2
Planning and Job Sequence

PLANNING

The best time to plan the basement layout is when the house is being built. Many houses today were obviously built with future basement use in mind: utility rooms such as laundry and storage are set up in remote corners; bathroom plumbing is roughed in; heating and air conditioning appliances are located so one can plan and utilize remaining space for maximum use and advantage.

But, it doesn't require extensive detective work to learn that most basements were built with no thought given to future expansion. Stairways are poorly located, so they not only cut up space and make it unworkable, but also make moving materials and appliances into the basement almost impossible. Furnaces may be set smack dab in the middle of the basement, making it impossible to lay out any large, uninterrupted spaces for game or recreation rooms. Floor drains are badly located so one must break up large portions of the concrete floor in order to install shower or bathroom waste drains. The first order of planning must be to overcome or correct bad layout by the original builder.

Someone has observed that good housing design is timeless, because it makes the space "work." How many times have you said to yourself that a door in your house is in the wrong place? Or the stairs are too steep, or too narrow, for comfortable use? Have you ever tried to cook in a really badly planned kitchen? Then you know the importance of good design. If you're not sure of your own design, have a builder or architect take a look at the plan before you proceed. Keep in mind that good design will repay its cost not only by enhancing the value of the property, but also by enhancing the livability of the space on a daily basis. The reverse is also true: there is a price that is extracted by bad design, and you will pay that price in daily installments as you occupy the space.

ACCESS

As mentioned elsewhere, poor stairway location can be a very negative factor in remodeling or using basement space. If you intend to use the basement, or a portion of it, for play space for your children and their friends, poor stairway location can turn your main floor living space into a raceway, as children move between their upstairs bedrooms and the basement play area. If the basement will be used as a recreation room for adult or family parties, do you really want all guests to move through the kitchen, en route to the basement, while you are trying to prepare food? Think about the extra traffic you will create, and how the present stairway location will work for that new traffic flow, before you decide that the stairway is workable in its present location.

Moving a stairway to a new location admittedly will increase the scope and cost of your basement project. Before you decide, have a contractor advise you on how feasible moving the stairway would be, and what it would cost. Moving a stairway involves cutting through the floor for a new stairway opening, installing and modifying joist headers to support the altered floor, and closing up the old stairway location. Although it is not a terribly hard job to do, it does involve making changes that affect the structural integrity of the house, so the job is one that requires expert knowledge.

Access Alternatives

You should consider access requirements both for convenience and for safety. Your local building code may require a secondary exit from finished basement space. Whether codes require it or not, you should be sure your basement has at least one optional exit, in case of fire or other emergency. Even an oversized window, one that is large enough for adults to climb through, is sufficient in most cases. Because most house fires occur at night, when sleeping occupants of the house may not notice early warning signs of fire such as odors or smoke, a secondary exit is mandatory if the new basement remodel contains bedrooms or sleeping accommodations such as convertible sofas for use of occasional guests.

If the existing stairway location does not complicate the basement floor space for room layout, consider installing a circular stair instead of moving the existing one. A circular stair can be an architectural attraction, one that adds a focal point of interest, just as a fireplace does. The installation of a circular stair in addition to the ex-

isting stair can permit you to redirect traffic, so that people do not have to pass through occupied space to get to the basement. Installing a circular stair near the entrance of the home can permit guests to go directly to the party.

Circular stairs can be installed in as little as 3' or 4' square areas, so they don't take up much floor space. Keep in mind, however, that circular stairs with limited diameters are designed for live traffic only, and are not wide enough to permit passage of furniture or building materials.

Another option would be to install a basement access door from the outside. Units such as the Bilco Basement Door (see photos) can provide easy access for moving in appliances, workshop tools or materials, and for storing seasonal items such as yard and lawn tools and furniture. Stopping traffic through the house, and the tracking of dirty, wet footprints across floors, should be a prime motivator in deciding to install an outside entrance.

Installing the outside door is a job for a masonry contractor, as the photos may suggest. The job includes excavating the lawn at the door location, cutting through the concrete wall, installing base drain tile and footings, laying up a concrete block wall, then installing the risers, the steps and the entry door at the basement wall. Then the steel door/cover must be installed atop the stairs and finished to suit.

Other options to open up the basement include bumping out the concrete wall and installing a greenhouse roof atop the bumpout. This can be an incredible addition because it takes away that claustrophobic feeling of being underground, and the natural lighting that is admitted by the enlarged window area can eliminate the need for artificial lighting in daylight hours. Installing operable roof windows in your bumpout can eliminate moisture problems as well. Circulating outside air into the finished basement can eliminate fear of mold and mildew and the musty odors that attend

Contractor lays concrete block in outside door excavation. Bilco Co. also has stringers that can be attached to concrete walls to hold steps. Photo courtesy Bilco Co.

The finished job shows steel doors that swing up to provide convenient access to the basement from outdoors. Properly installed, the doors offer weatherproof cover, plus complete security with handy access. Photo courtesy of Bilco Co.

To install basement door, contractor excavates stair path to the foundation with a tractor-mounted backhoe. Photo courtesy of Bilco Co.

Contractor uses a masonry saw to cut through the concrete foundation wall to make an entry door. Photo courtesy of Bilco Co.

these problems, so you should consider the value of added ventilation when deciding whether the project is worth the price.

BATHROOM

Few amenities you can add are as useful and valuable as an extra bathroom, and if you are planning to use the basement space as full-time living space a bathroom is mandatory. The basement bath can be a half-bath, or a stool and lavatory that will require only a 4′ × 4′ space. The half-bath alone should save a lot of traffic between floors, plus saving the attendant wear and tear. If you have an active family that is involved in many sports, a basement level shower can help reduce the cleaning chores on your main bathroom. If hot-tubbing is your game, an expanded bath that can hold an oversized whirlpool makes sense. Options include deep Japanese soak tubs that resemble a barrel — tubs with sidewall seating built in so you can actually be in hot water right up to your neck. Other options are exercise room, dressing room(s), and built-in sauna. You must allow extra room for all options, and you may have to install either an extra water heater to handle all that volume, or a large-capacity (commercial rating) water heater. You can use masking tape or duct tape to lay out appliance locations on the floor, so you can get a visual idea of the scope of each project and how it will impact on your overall basement plan.

As you start your plan, do a preliminary layout on graph paper, so everything is planned to scale. As the plan progresses you can add or subtract space between rooms, as needed. For minimum distances between bathroom fixtures, see the Plumbing section in Chapter 7. Note that these are minimum distances and comfort and convenience will be increased if space available permits a more roomy layout.

As you proceed with your scale layout, consider exactly what you will use the space for. If you find yourself short of space, try to make a room do

double-duty by better planning. Suppose you use exercise equipment three days per week, for thirty-minute workouts. This would mean you need exercise space for 1½ hours weekly, hardly enough time to dictate devoting an entire room to exercise. By contrast, let's assume a family of six who are all "jocks": the exercise then becomes a major activity that would demand committed space for the necessary equipment.

To avoid mistakes and confusion during the building stage, you must stick with the planning until you have scale working drawings hammered out. Your building department will demand working drawings before issuing building permits; but beyond this requirement is the need to have a plan with checkoff points so you don't overlook things. The working plans will also save you much time and many miles of "gofer" trips, preventing you from having to "gofer" this and "gofer" that because you have forgotten materials or tools needed. A solid plan will also help you arrive at a concrete dollar cost for your project, so you won't have any budget surprises.

As you plan, look ahead to the next section, Job Sequence, and Chapter 3, SPACE SAVERS AND ORGANIZERS. These will help you plan the flow of the job, and will help you organize space to free ore area up for your project. Also, before you finalize the plan, consider the suggestions in Chapter 11, N0-MESS OPTIONS, which discusses using prefinished materials to reduce finishing time and also reduce the dust, odors, and mess that so often become a factor in remodeling jobs.

JOB SEQUENCE

A common error for homeowners who decide to do their own contracting is to schedule or perform jobs out of sequence. Taking a logical approach to remodeling will help you avoid extra work and extra expense as the job progresses.

An example might be that of the couple who found

Flexibility is the name of the game when planning family recreation space. This basement retreat has wood paneling for warmth and easy maintenance. An exercise nook in one corner, at left, holds an exercise bike, weights or rowing machine, and keeps them out of the way for traffic while offering a full view of the room. At right an electronic entertainment center holds a TV, VCR and stereo equipment. Photo courtesy of Plywood Paneling Council.

a carpet remnant on sale and brought it home for the basement. They installed the carpet, then found a similar bargain in paneling for the wall. They lugged the paneling home, nailed it in place, and felt they were progressing nicely with their recreation room. Some time later they called the contractor and asked him to install a wallboard ceiling and finish it with a spray texture. The problem was that the ceiling should have been the first step, then the wall paneling (so the paneling could cover the cracks around the perimeter of the wallboard ceiling). It is impossible to finish a ceiling against the walls, because it will always crack. The contractor suggested using molding to cover the crack, but the couple objected, saying they wanted a clean corner line, without molding. The contractor then asked whether they had done the electrical wiring before nailing the paneling in place. Nope, they thought they would worry about the wiring at some later date. When the contractor pointed out they had reversed the order in which jobs are normally scheduled, the couple became hostile. They could not see that the ceiling, being the messiest job, should logically have been done first. Why place paneling on the wall, and carpeting on the floor, and then plaster and spray texture? It only requires extra effort to protect the finished products in place from being damaged or destroyed by being covered with dust, wallboard compound, and spray from the texture operation. You do not want carpet on the floor when you are moving building materials about, or spraying paint. In building as in other matters, there is to everything a season.

Because part of the project is in place when you are finishing off existing space, project sequence varies somewhat from building a new house or addition. For example, all framing is done in new construction, then the mechanical jobs such as wiring and plumbing are done. But in a basement remodel it would be better to break up the concrete floor and add needed floor drains, then patch the concrete floor, before framing any partitions that might be

in the way when you install the drain. For example, plan where the bathroom will be, break up the floor, install sewer drain pipes, patch the trench in the floor where you laid the drain pipes, then build the walls of the bathroom.

Similarly, one would normally do all the framing before installing electrical wiring. But, if you are furring out a concrete wall and installing foam board insulation such as Styrofoam®, you should run Romex™ wire to the spot where you need an electrical outlet, fasten the wires to the outlet box, and leave the wiring hang until you reach that spot in your furring job. Then install the furring strip, nail or staple the outlet box to the wood furring strip, then cut the foam board insulation to fit around the box and install the insulation.

Likewise, plan carefully for the job sequence where you will install any large components such as fiberglass tub/shower units, hot tubs, etc. It is best to place them on the site where they will be installed, so you won't have to remove wall studs to get them into the bathroom if they can't be fitted through a door. This may sound elementary, but I once had to remove a wall because the owner had pushed an old-style upright piano into a corner, where it would be out of the way while he was framing. He remembered that he did not want the piano to be permanently located in the back bedroom only after he had already installed the wallboard, and found he could get the piano through the bedroom but could not turn it down the hall because the hall was only 3 feet wide.

The key is, don't overlook anything during the planning stage. Do you plan to install a stereo system later, but don't have the money to do it now? It will cost very little to go ahead and do the wiring for remote speakers now, and you can easily install the expensive components later as you can afford them. It costs very little to have the telephone wiring done, or to do it yourself, with extra phone jacks at any conceivable location where they might be needed. But do it before you install wallboard

TELEPHONE LIST
SUPPLIERS & SUBCONTRACTORS

Supplier/Subcontractor Name	Contact	Phone	Bid Amount
Lumber Yard: RIDGE BLDRS SUPPLY	MARK MORRIS	555-4900	
Home Center: SAME			
Decorating:			
Plumbing:			
Electrical:			
Heating:			
Contractor:			
Excavator:			
Plumber: BROWN, INC.	ED BROWN	555-1821	$1580⁰⁰
Electrician: ACE ELECTRICAL	JANET MATTHEWS	555-0510	900⁰⁰
Drywall: COHEN DRYWALL	RAY COHEN	555-2886	964⁰⁰
Painter:			
Paperhanger:			
Bldg. Dept.:	LOU BOLEN	555-1759	
Inspectors:	PAM HITCHCOCK	555-0181	
	EARL WILLOUGHBY	SAME	
OTHER:			

or paneling, and then have to "fish" the wiring through very difficult paths to do the job.

The normal job sequence then is to do all the framing, but use the foresight we mentioned regarding plumbing and running needed heating pipes or ducts. After all framing is installed do the electrical and plumbing rough-in work. At this point you should also make any alterations to the heating duct system, or run hot water pipes if you have radiant heating. Don't overlook other mechanical projects such as telephone or stereo wiring. In addition to electrical service outlets, complete wiring for lighting. Check your plan for odd wiring requirements, such as wiring for lighting over pictures, or wiring for lighting in china, trophy, or gun cabinets.

When you have completed all mechanical projects, install batt insulation. A common problem is to be careless in fitting batt insulation. Any voids or careless fits around electrical outlets or pipes render the insulation ineffective. Insulation must present an uninterrupted barrier to be efficient.

Don't forget to insulate in special areas. Packing insulation in holes where pipes penetrate through framing can help reduce plumbing noises from pipes banging. Apply a layer of insulation board or Sound Stop board, available in 4' × 8' panels, over plumbing walls of bathrooms to stop bathroom noises from penetrating into bedrooms or recreation rooms. Also use acoustic measures to prevent party noises from recreation rooms from penetrating into adjoining sleeping rooms, or into the living space above.

When the insulation is completed, apply the wallboard. If you want paneling as a finish material on the walls, you should apply a layer of ⅜"-thick wallboard to serve as a base on which to attach paneling.

When wallboard is in place, apply three finish coats (see Chapter 8, with wallboard). Complete all wallboard finishing and allow it to dry. Inspect the wallboard job with a strong sidelight (a bare 100 watt bulb in a trouble light or in a shadeless lamp). Only after all messy or dusty parts of the wallboard project are finished should you move other materials into the workplace.

When the wallboard is finished and the ceilings are spray textured, the walls primed, you can begin the application of doors and trim. Doors are installed before baseboard, and the door and vanity must be in place before you install any ceramic tile in the bathroom. Then the tile can be fitted against the door trim, the sides of the vanity cabinet, and against the countertop.

Finish installing the clothes poles and shelving in the closets. Don't overlook the closet organizers that double the use of closet space.

Install any wainscoting or paneling as desired. Install other items such as desks, bars, or cabinet.

When the trim work is all done, do any staining and varnishing. Then apply the finish coat of paint to the walls. Do all painting before installing the final finish materials such as carpeting.

If you plan a suspended acoustic ceiling, the ceiling goes in last, after wallboard is finished and painted. This sequence avoids having finished material in place during the messy jobs.

Any ceramic floor tiling in the bathroom must be in place and grouted before you set the plumbing fixtures. Other floor finishes, such as vinyl sheet goods or carpeting, are done last. This is to avoid traffic from other building trades on new carpet or vinyl. Ceiling light outlets, for example, may have to be cleaned if they have wallboard compound in them. It is best to install lighting fixtures before you install floorcovering so that dust from the wallboard does not fall on the flooring.

At each step, try to plan the work flow so that work already done is not a hindrance to work yet to

PROJECT GUIDE

Planning	**Notes**
DECIDE on use of space	*FINALIZE BY 5/1*
LAY OUT room dimensions on floor	
INSPECT concrete walls for cracks	
INSPECT joists and existing framing for alignment	
DRAW working plan to scale	*CALL DAVE FOR HELP ON THIS*
MAKE multiple copies of plan	
SUBMIT plans to Building Department	*BY 5/15*
SUBMIT plans for bids, estimates	
MAKE supplier, contractor choices	*ASAP AFTER BLDG. DEPT OKs*
PATCH and waterproof concrete walls, floors	
FRAME walls, install backing	
ROUGH-IN plumbing	
ROUGH-IN electrical, phones	
ROUGH-IN heating	
INSTALL fireplace	
CALL for first inspection	*555-0181*
INSULATE	
INSTALL vapor barrier	
INSTALL wallboard, tile board	
TAPE and finish wallboard	
PRIME wallboard	
TEXTURE ceilings	
INSTALL paneling	
FINISH closet interiors	
INSTALL vanity, cabinets	
TRIM, install doors	
SET ceramic tile	
PAINT, stain	
INSTALL electrical devices	
SET plumbing fixtures	
FINISH electrical, hang lighting	
HANG wallcovering	
CLEAN rooms, floors	
LAY carpet	
CALL for final inspection	

come. For example, all switches and electrical receptacles should be installed after wallboard is finished and painted, so you won't mess the electrical equipment with wallboard compound or paint. Think each stage of the work through before you begin.

BUILDING PERMITS

Most cities require that you get a building permit for any remodeling work, additions, or alterations to your home. Check with the Inspections Division of your local building department to find what permits you must obtain. Most communities insist that you buy a permit for the overall project, in addition to getting special permits for any changes or additions to the home's mechanical systems. These separate permits usually include permits for any changes in the electrical, plumbing, and heating systems. Often, the Inspections Division can provide information that will assist you in planning your project.

The reasons for getting building permits and necessary inspections are often obscure to the homeowner. Many homeowners view the permit system as being just another way for the government to extract taxes from the individual. And, it is certainly true that the cost of building permits has risen in the past two decades. So why not just "bootleg" the remodeling job in, when it can't be detected from outside the house?

The first reason for obeying inspection and permit rules is that it is illegal not to do so. Beyond the illegality and possible legal consequences are more threatening penalties. Note the requirement for separate permits for the mechanical systems: electrical, heating, and plumbing. Mistakes made in changing these systems can be life-threatening, not only to your own family, but to neighbors who live nearby. People who do their own remodeling often enlist the help of the relative who swears he is an expert in electrical work. Are you sure you want

to accept this free labor uninspected? What if your uncle the expert proves not to know about things electrical, and you have a house fire from a short? My advice is to obey permit and inspection requirements.

There is yet another consideration for obeying permit laws. You may find that your insurance company can refuse payment for damages to your house, caused by illegal alterations. You may put your house and family in jeopardy, and void any claims to your insurance, if the house is damaged by fire and the cause is found to be illegal electrical work. In the same vein, consider the consequences if the fire in your house spreads to your neighbor's house. You are liable at law for damages to others that are a direct cause of your negligence. Don't take such a risk to avoid the fee, usually a couple of hundred dollars, that permits would cost.

Suppose you decided not to comply with permit requirements, and you find the threat of possible fire or explosion from electrical and plumbing mistakes to be too remote to consider. Suppose you get away with avoiding permit costs, and the day comes when you decide to sell your dream home. Suppose also that the prospective buyer decides he likes your house, and brings in a house inspector to determine the house's condition. If that inspector notes code violations in your do-it-yourself electrical job, he may advise that you be forced to bring in a licensed electrician to bring the thing up to code. Now you are stuck with delays, possible tear-out to open up walls or ceilings for workmen or inspectors, and high repair costs. Your buyer may just decide to move on, rather than risk getting a lemon. If this scenario seems far-fetched, consider that home buyers are increasingly being advised to bring in professional inspection services. And consider that these professional inspectors list bungled home projects as among the most common causes of problems with code compliance inspections at sale time.

JOB SCHEDULE

Project	Materials Bought	Date Begun	Date Finished	Inspected
Framing	5/22	5/24	5/30	
Electrical, rough		6/2	6/5	/
Plumbing, rough		6/3	6/5	/
Heating		6/2	6/7	6/10
Insulation	5/22	6/11	6/12	
Wallboard	6/8	6/15	6/21	
Wallboard, finishing				
Trim				
Ceramic tile				
Painting				
Wallcovering				
Suspended ceilings				
Finish lighting fixtures				
Floorcovering				
Set fixtures, plumbing				

INSPECTIONS

Ask your local building office for a copy of their inspection guidelines. The basic rule is that you will call for inspections at certain stages of the job. For example, the inspector will check your framing work to be sure that you have done nothing to alter the structure that could weaken it.

For mechanical work such as electrical wiring, plumbing, and heating, you must call for inspection as soon as the rough-in stage is completed. Rough-in for electrical work is when the wires (usually Romex™) are run, and secured into outlet boxes. The electrical work gets final inspection when the fixtures are installed.

For plumbing, rough-in is when the water supply, drain, waste, and vent pipes are installed. As with the electrical work, plumbing final inspection is due when the fixtures are installed.

Any alterations or additions to your heating system must also be inspected. This is to ensure that you do not have dangerous conditions such as leaking gas lines, or improper electrical wiring, that could cause a fire or explosion.

It is essential that you do not proceed with other projects until inspections are complete. This is especially true of electrical inspections, because the inspector must approve the job and sign off on an inspection tag. He or she will want to inspect the job with all your work visible and accessible. You cannot install insulation, wallboard, or paneling that would prevent the inspector from viewing the complete job. He or she can — and often will — order you to remove any material that covers up electrical work that has not been inspected and approved. For more information and sample permits on the mechanical trades, see Chapter 7.

SAMPLE PERMIT
BUILDING PERMIT APPLICATION

Date _____

Owner _____ Address _____

Phone _____ _____
City   Zip

Contractor _____ Address _____

Phone _____ _____
City   Zip

Job Site Address _____

Nature of work _____

Remodel _____ Addition _____ Demo _____ Move _____ New Const. _____ Repair _____

Total Square Feet of Proposed Building: _____ Overall Size: _____

Basement: Full _____ Partial _____ Crawl Space _____ Slab _____ Plans Submitted: YES _____ NO _____

Garage Size: _____ Detached _____ Attached _____

RE-ROOF: # of Sq. Ft. of Material _____ Tear Off: _____ Weight of Shingles _____
(yes/no)

RE-SIDE: # of Sq. Ft. of Material _____ Type of Siding _____

(F COMMERCIAL OR MULTI. RESIDENTIAL, SUBMIT SPECIFICATIONS FOR RE-ROOF OR RE-SIDE)

** SPECIAL NOTE: SEPARATE PERMITS SHALL BE OBTAINED FOR PLUMBING, ELECTRICAL, HEATING, VENTILATING, AND AIR CONDITIONING INSTALLATIONS.

Valuation of Job: To include plumbing, electric, ventilating, heating, and air conditioning costs.

ESTIMATE VALUATION OF THE JOB:

$ _____

Applicant's Signature

_____

Phone: _____

☐ BUILDING PERMIT FEE _____

☐ PLAN CHECK FEE _____

☐ STATE SURCHARGE _____

☐ S.A.C. CHARGES _____

☐ SPECIAL INVEST. FEE _____

TOTAL _____

PLEASE MAKE CHECKS PAYABLE TO: _____

3
Space Savers and Organizers

When you begin to plan your basement and how you will use the space, you may find there are fewer options than you thought. The utility room where the furnace and water softener sit is necessary space; so too is the laundry area with the washer, dryer, double laundry tubs, ironing board, and sorting table. And, the workshop area has to be preserved. Where else can we put grandpa's old wood lathe and floor-standing drill press? Then there's the ping-pong table, used to stack dirty clothes bound for the laundry . . .

If the above scenario sounds like home, you've got to rethink your priorities. The first rule, as someone once observed, is never love anything that can't love you back. Get rid of everything that is useless, or waiting to be fixed (if it has been waiting more than one year, you might consider the cause lost) or perfectly good but never used.

De-junk the place, and throw all the junk away. This means outgrown clothes, old magazines, newspapers, broken lamps of statues with clocks in their navels, discarded toys and sporting goods. If the stuff is worthless, put it in the pile.

The second pile is for usable items that *you* don't use. Exercise bicycles, ping-pong tables, shop tools and any other items that are in workable condition but unused by your family should go in this pile. Have a garage sale to help pay for your remodeling, or give game or toy items to children's centers or church youth groups. Reduce the basement clutter to only those things that are used.

Next, after you de-junk, plan how you could increase the usable space. Laundry equipment and organizers are so compact today that you can move them into a closet. The old double laundry tubs have been eliminated: today the clothes washer drains its water into a standing drain pipe. With a slight change in plumbing you could reduce the laundry space to near zero. Better still, you might consider moving the laundry into a spare closet (is there such a thing?) in the bedroom area, or into the bathroom closet, or even, if you live in a warm climate, into the corner of the garage.

And, the workshop. Donate unused tools to workshops for the elderly, or to vocational groups that train teenagers. In some instances you can take a tax deduction for your overflow items, or it might be reward enough just to be rid of the clutter. If you are not a workshop buff, and your workshop is dedicated only to repair and maintenance (at least after you've finished the basement) take advantage of the workshop organizers available to

This stackable laundry pair from Sears fits in any closet, lets you move the laundry room into the bathroom, master bedroom suite, or a hall closet, so you can remove the laundry from the basement and use the space for other purposes. Photo courtesy of Sears.

This combination washer/dryer fits in any space, takes up the same area as a single appliance would. If you want to keep a basement laundry but can't spare all that room, this laundry center could solve your problem. Photo courtesy of Sears.

Laundry organizers by Closet Maid include handy clothes pole for hanging clothes fresh from the dryer, shelves to hold laundry supplies. Over-appliance shelving can free up space needed elsewhere. Plan your needs and design laundry storage especially for your space. Photos courtesy of Clairson International.

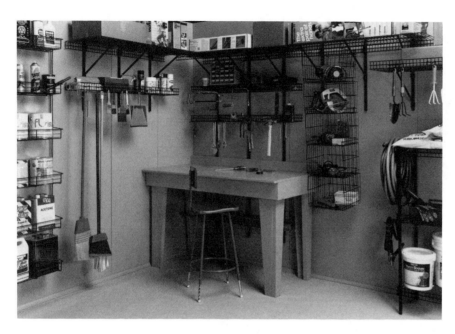

Wall-hugging workshop bench and organizers won't take up much space in your basement. Note wall shelving with hanging pegs on edges. If this still takes up too much basement space, fit these shop helpers along the end or side walls in the garage, or put the shop in a storage shed. Photo courtesy of Clairson International.

If you're a woodworker or hobbyist with limited work-space, check out the benchtop power tools available, such as this scroll saw. Photo courtesy of Sears.

shrink the space needed to a minumum. You can fit a do-it-all workshop into a few feet of floor space or a small corner, if you plan wisely.

Don't overlook space-efficient tools now available if you're reducing workshop size. Condo and townhouse living has grown over the past decade or more, and this has inspired tool companies to design power tools on a smaller scale. Many tools that formerly were available only as floor-standing models now are made to fit on the workbench. And, they're not playthings: some of the bench-toppers have all the power and capacity you'll need for anything short of a boatyard. Nor are you limited to just a few spacesavers that will fit under the workbench when not being used. In a shelved area the size of an ordinary linen closet you can store a half-dozen or more of these economy-sized tools.

CLOSETS AND STORAGE

No area of the house has gotten anywhere near the attention that has been given to closet and storage space in the past decade. The reasons are fairly obvious: we are just buying more stuff. Where our parents had neither the leisure time nor the money to invest in tons of sporting gear, most families today not only are involved in many sports, fashion now decrees that each sport have its own costume. Leotards for aerobics, jogging suits for chasing dogs through the park, basketball and volleyball and hockey in winter — and a full set of clothing for each sport. The entire storage/organizer industry is the result of our fitness craze.

Those who design these organizers have left no area untouched. The space formerly vacant, over the water closet (tank), now can be fitted with shelving or cabinets designed for just that space. Likewise the blank space that we used to see above the washer and dryer now has storage for many cubic feet of miscellaneous gear. Not to mention the improvements made in space that was actually intended for storage: closets can now be custom-designed by the homeowner, each shelf and hanger

to fit your own inventory of clothes, shoes, luggage, and the like.

To help you plan exactly the space you need, and use the space to the maximum, browse through the storage/organizer department of a discount or department store. You will find door-length shoe racks that hold dozens of pairs of shoes, storage drawers with casters that can be rolled away under the bed or into closets. Most of these storage units appear tailor-made for basement use: the vinyl-covered steel racks, baskets and shelves are colorful, decorative, and are open-air for good circulation. This last point cannot be stressed too strongly: the days of mildew and musty odors went out with the organizers.

The final point about the organizer craze is that you don't need instruction to build these shelves and storage units, and there is no painting or finishing to be done. You can measure your own space, shop for organizers you need, bring them home, and fasten them up, all in the time it would take a carpenter to unpack his tools. If the time comes when you don't need them, or prefer to use them elsewhere, they're easily moved with no more effort than plugging up the old screwholes and driving new screws where you need the storage.

Double-duty Space

We've explored making maximum use of available space via reorganizing it. But there are other space-savers to consider before you lock in your new basement plan.

The photos showing the wall bed should illustrate the point. With the bed folded into the wall unit, the floor space is free for use as a recreation area, a game room, an entertainment center, with another wall fitted with shelves for electronic gear such as the TV and VCR.

Move a couple of chairs or a coffee table and the bed can fold down to transform the space into a guest bedroom, or a teenager's retreat. The wall units are available also with such built-ins as book-shelves, or desk space for study or for keeping family accounts.

Or, you can fold the bed back into the wall, pull the dumbbells or exercycle out of a storage closet, plug in your aerobics videotape, and the room becomes an exercise spa.

MIRRORS

Don't overlook mirrors and the role they can play in room expansion. Decorators have always used mirrors to make a space seem larger than it is. Mirror tile installed above a bar or snack area can expand the space visually; mirror doors on closets dramatically alter the feeling of spaciousness in a small room. In one room I know of, originally the mid-sized of three bedrooms in a townhouse, a 10′ × 12′ room was fitted with mirrored closet doors, floor to ceiling. A youth bed was removed and replaced by a sofa bed; a TV set was mounted at eye level on a corner bracket. The room thus became a multi-purpose space that was at once a guest bedroom, a TV den, and, with the addition of a bookcase, a library retreat.

Home office for recordkeeping or homework fits into corner of any room. Steel shelving is easily moved, completely adjustable. Photo courtesy of Clairson International.

Rolling cart has wide casters for easy travel over carpet, can be rolled under shelving, into closet when not in use. This is a perfect organizer for students or for home office. Photo courtesy of Clairson International.

Any corner becomes a closet with adaptable, adjustable shelving. Open shelving, whether used inside or outside of closet, is perfect solution to avoid humidity problems with stored items. Stackable wire baskets permit air circulation, prevent musty odors. Photo courtesy of Clairson International.

Tennis anyone? Hanging wire baskets store sporting goods, eliminate clutter in teenager's room. Photo courtesy of Clairson International.

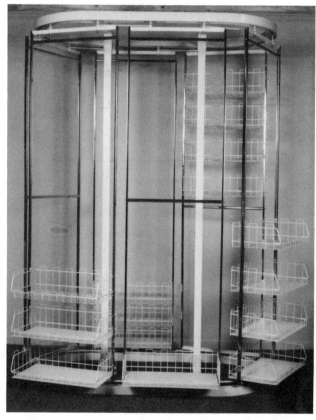

Closet Maid Revolving Closet™ offers large clothes storage capacity in a small area. This revolving rack lets you parade your entire wardrobe by, while you stand in one spot. The ultimate in convenience and accessibility for clothes storage. Photos courtesy of Clairson International.

Closet Maid says that if your shoes are on the floor they should be on your feet. This vertical door storage rack fits on a closet door. Shoe storage lets you free up floor space while keeping shoes clean and organized. Photo courtesy of Clairson International.

A dry, airy corner of the basement can be converted to locker-type, overflow storage. Store off-season clothing or sporting gear here; change contents of bedroom closets and storage closet as seasons and clothing demands change. The ultimate: Line the walls and ceilings with aromatic cedar. Photo courtesy of Clairson International.

Wallbeds permit multiple uses for space. A recreation room can double as a spare or guest bedroom with the foldaway bed. Above, the bed and desk unit are closed and the space can be used for daytime activities. With the desk open it becomes a family finance center for handling bills or correspondence. With the chair removed and the bed folded down, the space converts to a sleeping room. Photos courtesy of Sico Co.

4
Tools and Equipment

There's an old adage in the building trades that states: "By the tools you will know the workman." You simply cannot do a quality job without the proper tools. Most journeymen buy the best tools they can find. Why make a job more difficult by refusing to invest in tools that are designed especially to fit the difficult task? If you've ever tried to remove a faucet assembly with just any wrench that is handy, rather than using a basin wrench designed for the job, you know what we mean. Experience and know-how are great, but having the right tool is more than half the battle.

With that in mind, the first advice to the homeowner is: don't try to make do with whatever tools are in your kit. Buy, borrow, or rent specific tools to do the job right. If it doesn't make sense to invest in the tools to do a project, hire it done. In fact, many projects boil down to just that point: the job may be so complicated, and the tools so expensive, and your (future) need for them so limited, that it only makes sense to call a pro.

TOOL RENTAL

One alternative to buying expensive tools for one-time use is to rent the tool. Rental equipment stores in major cities offer everything from backhoe tractors for digging your own basement to rotary sewer cleaners like the pros use. Your problem is to decide whether you have the expertise to use the tool after paying the rental, or if hiring a pro makes sense. Not everyone can clean a sewer and walk away with a clean uniform, just because they have the right equipment.

The best way to decide whether to rent the tool or hire a pro is to get a bid from the pro, and check the rental cost at the store. Renting tools can be expensive, because the job invariably will take more time than you estimate. Those half-day rental rates that are quoted by tool rentals can be misleading because you seldom can do a job and get the tool returned within a four to six hour period.

The first rule, if you decide to rent, is to be very sure that the job has reached the stage where the rental tool is the next step. You do not want to pay rental rates while the tool lies unused. The second rule is to finish the job and return the tool immediately. If you leave the tool lying about instead of returning it, you pay a heavy penalty for the delay.

Tools You Can Rent

Tools you might consider renting for basement finishing include:

- 10-lb. sledge (for breaking concrete)
- Reciprocating saw (for cutting in difficult locations)
- Portable grinders (smoothing concrete floors, walls)
- Sanders
- Paint sprayer
- Angle drill (has 90° angle on chuck)
- Power hammer (uses powder charges to drive fasteners in steel, concrete)
- Miter saw (power or hand, for fine trim cuts)
- Texture machine (for spraying textures)

In addition to conventional tool rental firms, many specialty stores will rent or loan you the tools you need. For example, ceramic tile dealers usually will loan you the tools to install the tile you buy there; paint and wallcovering dealers loan wallcovering tools.

TOOL TIPS

Throughout this book, you will find tool lists for whatever job is described. The goal is to make the list useful, and to have a handy checklist to guide you in assembling the right tools before starting the job. This is intended to help you avoid that "7:00 p.m. Saturday" syndrome. That's the one where, at 7:00 p.m. on Saturday night, with one hour's work left to finish the job, you realize you don't have the tool(s) needed. The reason this always occurs at 7:00 p.m. on Saturday is because every hardware or tool store in the world closes at 6:00 p.m. Saturday.

If you want a general knowledge of tools, their uses and cost, and are starting your education at ground zero, your best route is to browse your favorite store's tool catalog. Those catalogs are far more comprehensive than this book could be. Or if you describe your project to the tool store clerk,

he should be able to tell you exactly what tool will do the job. What I'd like to do here is give you a few tips on tools that you won't find in most catalogs.

Chalk line — Consists of a teardrop-shaped chalk box, a mason's string, and a handle on the side for rewinding the strong (line). You buy powdered chalk at the tool store and fill the chalk box. Then, when you pull the line out of the chalk box it is coated with chalk. You either have a helper hold the pull on the end of the line or (if working alone) drive a temporary nail in the workpiece to clip the end to. Now, position the extended chalk line between the two points where you want a mark or cutline. With the chalk line pulled tight between the two points, and lying upon the material you want to mark, you pick up the line at some point between the ends, and let go of the line. The taut line will snap back against the material and leave a straight line, marked by chalk dust, on the material. The problem is that the line often leaves a heavy layer of the chalk dust, and the chalk is dirty. It gets on your clothes, and hands, and materials where you don't want chalk dust. If you leave the chalk on wallboard, for example, it will be picked up in your latex or other paint, and be carried all over the surface by the roller. Or, if you use the chalk line to mark the walls for installing a suspended ceiling, you will invariably get the chalk on your hands and spread it over the acoustic ceiling panels. **Cure:** Pull the line out of the box, and holding the line in the air, and away from any object you don't want marked, snap the line so the excess chalk flies off into midair. There will still be enough chalk left on the line to leave a mark, but not enough to make a mess on everything.

Hand saw — Go to the tool store and look for the "Good, Better, Best" saw selection. Buy the best. The quality saw will have a better handle and a blade of better steel. The better blade will be of high quality steel and will hold its sharpness longer than a cheap saw. The ease of cut with a hand saw depends on the sharpness of the teeth and the amount of *set* in the teeth. If a saw blade was simply notched to make teeth, it would be hard to use, because the cutting (teeth) edge of the saw would be the same width as the thickness of the saw blade. To open a saw cut or kerf slightly wider so the blade won't bind in the kerf, the saw's teeth are bent slightly, in alternate directions, to each side. Hold your saw with the cutting (teeth) side up and sight down the blade. You will see the set of the teeth. If the saw binds in the cut it probably needs to have the teeth sharpened and set. **Cure:** If the saw is new, or seems sharp, clean the blade with turpentine or odorless mineral spirits to remove any pitch or gum from the blade. If you are sawing much pine wood, clean the blade frequently. Don't drop the saw or permit it to bump against other metal tools that might dull the blade. If your sawhorse is tall enough so the tip won't touch the floor, hang the saw on a hanger that is fastened to the end of the sawhorse when using the saw. When not in use, you should hang the saw from pegboard hooks, with the cardboard blade cover in place, or secure a slotted wood piece over the toothed edge.

Circular saw — Keep a sharp blade in the saw. Circular saw blades are made with teeth designed for ripping (cutting with the grain), or crosscutting (cutting across the grain) or you can buy a combination blade for both purposes. A combination blade will serve for most homeowners because they are not doing that much ripping, and they don't like to be changing blades that often. For paneling, however, buy and use the multi-tooth paneling blades. The fine-tooth blades eliminate splintering of the face ply on paneling. Never force a circular saw (or any power tool). The side pressure when you force a saw puts pressure on the shaft and bearings. **Cure:** Invest thirty dollars in a top-of-the-line carbide-tipped blade.

Drill — A good all-purpose drill choice is the ⅜″ reversible, variable-speed drill. For heavy-duty boring rent or buy a ½″ drill. The modern variable-speed drills are a great improvement over the older, 1700 rpm models. High drill speeds are a detriment to using drills for anything but drilling; i.e., for mixing paint, or with polishing or buffing wheels. High drill speeds also will dull drill bits instantly when you are drilling in hard materials such as steel. **Cure:** When drilling steel or concrete, use the variable feature on your drill to keep the bit barely turning. Your impulse, when drilling in difficult material, is to open the drill speed to maximum. If the bit is not cutting, just spinning on the surface, it will overheat and dull quickly. This is why you see variable pulleys on a drill press: different materials require different drill speeds. Use carbide masonry bits when drilling in masonry.

Chisels — Accidents happen when you try to force a dull tool to cut. Keep a fine grinding wheel handy and keep chisels sharp. Don't use the wood chisel for any purpose but cutting wood. Don't drive a cold chisel (or any driven tool) with a carpenter's hammer: use a ball-peen or machinist's hammer. Use a wood or plastic mallet to drive wood chisels.

Hammers — Carpenter's hammers are made for driving and pulling nails. Do not use a carpenter's hammer as an all-purpose hammer. You can ruin a hammer by using it as a crowbar, or by driving chisels, star drills, or other hardened driving tools. Likewise, a carpenter's hammer is not heavy enough to drive hardened masonry nails: you may chip the face of your hammer, and the flying steel chip can injure an eye. Use a ball-peen or small sledge for driving hardened concrete nails and with driven tools. Keep the face of the hammer head clean: grease, wax, or the coating from nails can coat the hammer face, causing you to bend nails. **Cure:** Use a scrap of sandpaper to clean the hammer face frequently when you are working with adhesives, glues, coated nails, or any material that might coat the hammer face and cause it to slip when striking a nail.

Screwdrivers — Buy a variety of screwdrivers to cover all types and sizes of screws. At least three slot screwdrivers and three Phillips screwdrivers are necessary for ordinary household maintenance

Modern circular saws cut with less noise and vibration than older models, a welcome change for basement workshops. The 7¼" saw can be teamed with a variety of blades to handle any cutting job from wood paneling to cast iron pipe. Photo courtesy of Sears.

This compound miter saw has positive miter stops at 0°, 22½°, and 45°. The cast-iron base provides stability for accurate cuts. Ideal for trim, molding. Photo courtesy of Sears.

Sander/grinder is for rough projects only; shown here removing loose plaster from concrete block. Can be used with metal grinding blade also, or use adhesive-backed sanding discs for heavy-duty sanding projects. Photo courtesy of Sears.

For material removal or fine finishing, this palm sander is all the sander you will need for most finishing projects. Uses ¼ sheets of sandpaper, secured in place with level clamps. Photo courtesy of Sears.

This ⅜" electronic drill is reversing, variable-speed model. The best choice as an all-around home shop drill. If you haven't shopped for tools lately, look over new models: reduction in operating noise alone makes them a must for basement use where noise levels are important. Photo courtesy of Sears.

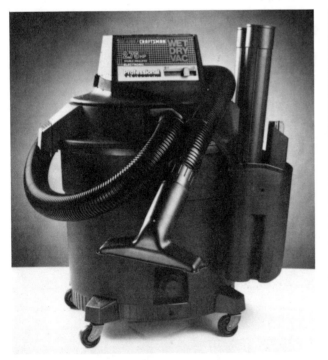

When the day's project is done, a wet/dry vac will ease the cleanup chores. This model rolls under the workbench, will hold 1.8 gallons of dry debris and 13 gallons of liquid. This vac has a bottom drain and automatic shutoff for liquid overflow. Use in basement, garage, shop, wherever there's a cleaning job. Photo courtesy of Sears.

and repair. Don't try to drive Phillips-head screws with a slot screwdriver: the screwdriver may slip and injure you, or damage the screw or the workpiece. The big advance in screwdrivers is the development of wallboard screw guns and wallboard (drywall) screws. The screws are available in many sizes and can be used for building and hanging cabinets, or installing door hinges, or for constructing almost any project from shelves to storage sheds. Be careful when working in damp places, where you might get a dangerous shock; and be careful also when you are using power tools on ladders or scaffold, where the cords can tangle underfoot and cause a fall. **Cure:** Choose a cordless, battery-powered drill to eliminate any danger from shock in damp work places, and to eliminate dragging an extension cord up a ladder. Cordless tools are a good investment in safety.

Razor knife — One tool that is included on most tool lists, whatever job you're doing, is the razor knife. Use it to cut wallboard, floorcovering, wallcovering, vapor barriers, insulation, building paper, and to sharpen your pencil. The problem is that cutting abrasive material such as the core in wallboard panels, or asphalt shingles, tends to dull the blade very quickly, and many people just will not throw those old blades away. You will work faster, be less tired, do a better job, and avoid tearing expensive materials such as wallcovering if you change the razor blade at each coffee break. **Cure:** Buy replacement blades for the razor knife in packages of 100 blades. Or, if throwing them away seems poor economy, carry a pocket whetstone in your tool bag and sharpen the blade a few times before you discard it.

Tool bags — If you do major remodeling work, invest in the pro-type leather tool bags. Some come already riveted to a web belt; some you will find loose in bins at cut rates. Buy the web canvas-type military belt, a nail (or screw) bag, and a tool holder. Rivet the two leather bags on the belt so they won't slip; the two bags should be worn so they are off the hip, not worn in front of your belly.

Nail and tool bags carried in your middle get in the way when you bend over. You can also injure yourself if you bend over with sharp tools carried in the range of your midsection. Don't overload the bags with nails, screws or tools: you'll have to carry that weight. **Cure:** If you must carry heavy tools, or you are slim-hipped and the bags won't stay put around your waist, attach a pair of canvas carpenter's suspenders to the belt to help support the weight.

T-square — Sometimes referred to as a wallboard T-square, this is one of the most useful tools you can own. If you do any cutting on wallboard, plywood, paneling, or any panel that is 4 feet wide, this tool is indispensable. The only warning is that you must avoid getting your free hand in the way when cutting along the T-square: if the knife slips you can get a nasty injury. **Cure:** When cutting panel material with the panels leaning against a wall, hold the top of the T with your free hand, keeping the hand well out of line of the knife cut. Place the toe of your work shoe against the bottom of the T to hold it from slipping sideways. Cut from the top down, halfway across the width of the panel. Now reverse the knife and cut from the bottom edge up, so you are pulling the knife away from, not towards, your foot. When using the T-square as a cutting guide for power tools, use a clamp to hold the T-square in place. This way, if the T-square or the saw or other cutting tool slips, you won't have a hand in the way.

Measuring tape — Cheap measuring tapes, or rules, are made for very infrequent use, and will not stand up to the wear and tear of a major remodeling job. Buy a tape that is at least 12′ long: 16′ or 25′ is better. Check the blade of the tape to be sure the measurements are clearly visible; you will often be working in poor lighting when remodeling. Buy a tape with a wide blade that will stand stiff when the blade is extended: ¾″ wide blades can be extended for measuring above your head, or down a wall, when you are working alone and don't have a helper to hold one end. Cheap tapes

Typical of the current crop of cordless tools is the adjustable torque screwdriver. The hex collet will accept any ¼″ driver bit. Handy storage compartment in the handle stores a variety of bits for fast retrieval. Photo courtesy of Sears.

Wallboard screw gun has adjusting collar that lets you control the depth of the dimple of the wallboard screw. Magnetic tips hold Phillips-head wallboard screws for easy handling. Photo courtesy of Gold Bond Building Products.

Cordless saber saw makes 45° bevel cuts and cuts flush vertically. A rip fence is included. Cordless tools prevent shocks, eliminate awkward extension cords that can snag and cause tool to miscut or become a tripping hazard for the worker. Photo courtesy of Sears.

Wallboard hatchet has large, crowned face to compress wallboard dimple without damage to wallboard. Offset (angled) handle protects knuckles. Photo courtesy of United States Gypsum.

have small or weak lips or hooks at the end: they either slip off the edge of the workpiece each time you try to extend the tape, or they break off easily. **Cure:** Check the end of the tape and be sure the lip is wide enough to stay hooked without slipping off the material, and is securely fastened to the tape blade.

Pencils — What could you possibly learn about using so common a tool as a pencil? Especially in trim carpentry where cuts and miters must be exact, the pencil you use and the way you use it is critical. Pick up a carpenter's pencil for marking framing lumber and sheathing plywood. The heavier pencil and lead will last much longer than an ordinary lead pencil when used to mark rough surfaces. But, for marking trim for cutting, the thickness of the pencil mark is crucial. You will often hear carpenters who work in pairs, with one person measuring and the other person cutting, say to "leave the mark" or "take the mark" when the cut is made. The saw blade itself can be ⅛″ thick, so even the width of a saw blade, when taken or left on either side of the pencil mark, can ruin a miter fit on trim. So, use a #2 lead pencil for marking dimensions on trim lumber, and keep the pencil sharp so you know *exactly* where the cut should be. **Cure:** For a super-sharp mark, screw a pencil sharpener to the underside of your workbench (so it's out of the way, not on the bench top) and sharpen the pencil frequently. Master trim carpenters go a step further: they also screw a pencil sharpener to the underside of the sawhorse that supports the miter saw, so they can put a fine point on the pencil after each cut.

Wallboard hammers — As stated in the wallboard chapter (Chapter 8), I urge anyone who is installing wallboard to use a screw gun, not a hammer, for driving the fasteners. The second-best advice would be: if you insist on nailing wallboard on, don't do so with a carpenter's hammer. The wallboard hammer is designed especially for that purpose and its advantages make it well worth the price. First, the wallboard hammer has a larger face than a carpenter's hammer, and the hammer's face is crowned or convex. This larger, crowned face lets you set the wallboard nail below the surface of the board, or dimple it, without crushing the plaster core around the nail, and without cutting the face paper around the perimeter of the hammer mark. These two factors — crushing the plaster core and cutting or fracturing the face paper — account for a large percentage of the fastener failure problems in wallboard. The wallboard hammer handle is longer than an ordinary carpenter's hammer handle, so you can reach the top portion of the 8 foot high wall while standing on the floor. Because you are working continually in contact with large panels, you also will be forever bumping your knuckles if you use a carpenter's hammer. **Cure:** Wallboard hammers have offset handles to protect knuckles.

Most basements can be finished using only hand tools, but stationary saws make the job easier. Radial arm (right) can be adjusted to cut miters or compound miters as required. With radial arm saw the workpiece stays stationary while the saw moves through the wood, rolling along on the overhead arm.

Below, the table saw has multiple adjustments for cutting trim, has depth adjustment up to 3⅜" (10" saw shown). The rip fence at left can be set so you can rip plywood sheets, 24" adjustment to left or right of the blade. Both saws offer better accuracy than cutting freehand; attachments for other functions such as sanding are available. Photos courtesy of Sears.

5
Materials

BUYING MATERIALS

If you live near a major building center, you may have already made your decision on where to buy your building materials. Still, it may be worth your while to take a complete materials list to a full-service lumber yard, one that caters to building contractors primarily, and ask them to bid your materials list. You may be able to arrange a contractor's discount when you are buying materials for a major job. In addition to price you may be able to negotiate delivery and charge privileges so you can pay monthly or at job's end.

Any contractor will tell you that there are major differences in the quality of building products. Some major merchandisers buy whatever product they can get in carload lots, for a low price, without regard to brand selection. Major brands very often became major because they offer the best product, and many lumber yards stock proven building products because they do not want the expense and customer dissatisfaction caused by callbacks. Ask your lumber dealer to help you select materials that are good quality and easy to work with.

Another point to consider is to decide early in the game what jobs you will do yourself, and what jobs you will have done by professionals. Pros are expected to guarantee their work, so most will want to supply materials needed for their particular job. Most contractors will balk at having to install any product they feel is substandard, for the obvious reason that they cannot guarantee something that the customer bought at a discount house. Also, a markup on materials is a part of the contractor's livelihood. Don't forget that a material markup is not all profit. The markup may include such things as shopping the item(s), paying the bills, hauling the materials to the jobsite, and unloading and placing the material. The contractor who furnishes materials must also absorb the cost of the waste and, depending on your contract, the cost of hauling away leftovers and debris.

MATERIAL DELIVERY

There are two factors to keep in mind when planning the timing for material deliveries. A common homeowner mistake is to bring the materials into the workplace prematurely. The materials are then in the way and are an obstacle to work progress. There are few things more frustrating than trying to apply compound to ceiling wallboard while tripping over a pile of flooring lumber stacked needlessly in the work path. Another problem is getting materials dirty. Paint spatters, dropped taping compound, and construction dust can easily ruin prefinished cabinets or fill the grooves on tongue-and-groove flooring, making it difficult to fit together. Finally, materials left in the workplace always become scratched and shopworn. Plan material deliveries so materials needed for the next phase of construction are not an obstacle to work in progress.

The other factor is that, while you don't want to stumble over materials, it is important that those materials be delivered so they can sit in the workplace for a few days to acclimate. To acclimate means to let materials reach an equilibrium with the temperature and humidity of the room. Building materials are often stored in unheated sheds, and if they are delivered cold from the lumber yard and immediately nailed in place, they may swell or shrink as they reach parity with the temperature and humidity in the workplace. Such products as wall paneling and hardwood flooring may either buckle as they expand or leave open joints as they contract, depending on their temperature and moisture content. The key is to let building products do their swelling and shrinking before you nail them in place, so they'll stay where you put them when installed.

Wood products are especially critical in the acclimation process, although manufactured wood products such as paneling are quite stable as they come from the factory. This is true because the moisture has been wrung out of these materials during the manufacturing process. By contrast, dimensional lumber such as framing lumber may have been kiln dried but may have picked up moisture during shipping or storage. It is a good idea to let most materials sit at least 72 hours in the work place before installing them. Let liquid or paste products such as paint and adhesives reach room temperature before applying them.

Inspect delivered materials for damage before accepting them. Wallboard, for example, is soft and is easily damaged by rough handling. Cracked panels or panels with broken edges or corners are difficult to finish, requiring both extra time and finishing materials. Uncrate cabinets and appliances and inspect them for shipping damage. Doing this inspection will reveal any damage or other problems immediately, so you can make claims for adjustment and/or replacement of the items. If you wait until you're ready to install materials before opening crates for inspection, your job may be delayed while you reorder, if you find the materials damaged or you've been sent the wrong color.

TOXIC MATERIALS

There has been a lot of news about possibly toxic building materials. Especially noted have been products containing formaldehyde and asbestos. The key points to consider here are that allergic reaction to building products varies widely with individuals. Just as some people are allergic to ragweed and some can sleep in the stuff, so reaction to various chemicals is an individual thing. A carpenter may work with plywood on a daily basis for twenty years and never suffer a reaction, while another person may react to the formaldehyde in particleboard furniture or in new carpeting.

The wood products industry, recognizing the concern of the public based on published reports, has reduced the use of urea formaldehyde by 90% in the past ten years. Also, formaldehyde levels drop rapidly in areas where good ventilation is provided. The industry and the Environmental Protection Agency suggest that you observe common sense procedures when remodeling. These procedures include:

● Provide full ventilation in the work area. This may include augmenting natural ventilation with fans, keeping doors and windows open or letting products sit in a garage or other open area to "air out" before bringing them into the house.

- Some people may react to new carpet. Unroll, or ask the installer to unroll, the carpet in a garage or on a deck or patio so it can air out before being laid.

- Choose paint and adhesives with care. In most cases latex-based paints and adhesives are less toxic than oil-based counterparts.

- Wear dust or particle masks to provide protection as needed. Avoid creating dust by using a wallboard wet sander and by using prefinished products such as paneling that have already undergone sanding and finishing at the factory.

- Provide as much ventilation as possible during and for several months after the job is completed. Maintain ventilation until the "new smell" is gone. If you experience any flu-like symptoms advise your physician that you are remodeling: flu symptoms are a common reaction to formaldehyde.

SHOPPING FOR HARD-TO-FIND MATERIALS

Fix-it books such as this one advise the reader to "seal the concrete," "clean off dirt and oil," "patch the concrete floor," "etch the concrete for better paint adhesion." The reader may often wonder: Where can I buy these miracle products? Half the time I can't find these wonder items, when I do find them, they don't work as claimed. So, here's a shopping hint for beginners.

Janitors' Supplies

Who knows more about tough cleaning jobs than a janitor in a school or factory? No one. So, when the pro has a tough cleaning job, he drops by the store where the professional janitor shops. You'll find the store listed in the Yellow Pages of your phone book under the heading "Janitorial Equip-

ment & Supplies." If your town is small and no such listing can be found, ask the janitor at your church, school, or the factory where you work.

The key to this advice is that caustic or corrosive materials that are manufactured for the consumer store shelf cannot be made extra duty. The concentration of the chemical is reduced to eliminate any hazard to homeowners who are unfamiliar with safety procedures, or who leave cleaning or building products about where children might get into them, or for those who just do not believe that any chemical caustic enough to remove heavy coats of old paint might also remove skin. Without wishing to get rank amateurs in too deep, I urge that you (1) buy a concentrated product that will get the job done; (2) read the labels, listen to the salesperson, and do not ignore safety rules for the product; (3) *always* wear protective gear such as eye goggles, rubber gloves, long-sleeved work shirts, over-the-ankle work boots for climbing or when lifting.

With those precautions in mind, what is your problem? Rust stains on the driveway or patio? Your janitorial supply has a chemical remover. Stucco, brick, or stone exterior is dirty? Ask your supply store for a masonry cleaner, and rent a power washer with enough pressure to remove the stain, or grime, or whatever.

Your janitorial supplier can recommend a professional quality concrete sealer. He can provide high-power, concentrated cleaners to remove oil, grime, efflorescence, or rust stains from concrete floors. Waxes, sealers, paints for rusting or other problem surfaces, window cleaners, concrete bonders, or just about any product you need to clean, protect, and/or maintain your house.

Another problem with shopping for materials is that often the part-time clerks in home centers don't know the products well enough to be of any help. I once sent an assistant out to buy some concrete bonding agent. After several hours he returned to tell me that no store in our vicinity carried the product. I went to the store and there it sat, some 200 gallons of it, wearing the label "Concrete Bonding Adhesive." The stuff looks like white latex paint, can be used to bond new concrete patches to the old damaged concrete, or can be used to make patches stick in plaster. Pros know this, and have used the stuff for decades: not only did the clerk know nothing of the product, he didn't even recognize the product when he was looking directly at it. In fairness to clerks, especially part-time help, there are a lot of products or SKUs (stock-keeping units) in the average store, and you have to spend some time to know them all. That is, of course, no help or consolation to the person needing the product. The only thing you can do is try to familiarize yourself with products you need, and keep asking. There is a product for nearly every purpose under the sun, so you have to keep asking until you meet the experienced person who knows how to help.

When All Else Fails

If you've tried every other source you know and still can't find a tool or product you need, visit where the pro shops. Got a plumbing problem? There are small plumbing shops, run by plumbers, who know everything about their trade. Have a problem with stains on brick? If you visit your library, you will find an array of books on the subject, plus an increasing array of videotapes that show you how to do almost anything. One helpful book, one you can buy for $10 or view free at your library, is the telephone book that lists toll-free 800 numbers for consumer companies that have an 800 number. Many companies list their 800 numbers on their product labels: Johnson Wax, for example, lists a consumer hotline 800 number on every product they make.

6
Framing and Insulation

TOOL LIST FOR FRAMING

- ☐ Hammer, 16 oz. carpenter's
- ☐ Hammer, 2 lb. mash or sledge
- ☐ Measuring tape, 25 ft.
- ☐ Circular saw, blades
- ☐ Plumb bob & chalk line combo
- ☐ Caulking gun
- ☐ Carpenter's square
- ☐ Combination square
- ☐ Carpenter's pencils
- ☐ Tool belt, nail bag
- ☐ Carpenter's level, 2-ft.
- ☐ Prybar
- ☐ Wallboard screwgun, screw selection
- ☐ Drill, assorted bits
- ☐ Utility knife, blades
- ☐ Extension cord(s)
- ☐ Crosscut (hand) saw
- ☐ 2″-wide masking tape (layout)
- ☐ Sawhorse(s), stepladder(s)
- ☐ Stud finder (electronic)
- ☐ Protective goggles
- ☐ Screwdrivers

FRAMING

Framing carpentry in a basement involves furring or framing exterior walls, setting interior partitions for rooms and closets, furring down or building soffits to cover pipes, heating ducts, or electrical conduit, and installing nailers or backing at the corners where walls meet walls or ceilings. Framing also involves building openings for room and closet doors. Because basement framing often involves not only fastening wood to wood, but also involves the more difficult jobs of fastening wood to steel (beams) or concrete, you will need to use exceptional tools and techniques.

Wood to Steel

Construction adhesives have been a real lifesaver for difficult fastening jobs. Choose an all-purpose construction adhesive for basement framing.

If you have a steel support beam running down or near the center of the basement ceiling, you may wish to position a wall directly under the steel beam. To fasten the top plate of the wall to the steel beam, choose a top plate that is wide enough to span the bottom flange of the I-beam.

Usually a 2 × 4 will span the flange width, but for

heavier beams you may need a 2 × 6. Whatever your plate width, apply a liberal bead of adhesive to the top side of the plate, the side that will fit against the bottom of the I-beam. Use large C-clamps to clamp the top plate to the steel beam. Now (wearing protective goggles) use a 9/64″-diameter bit in a ⅜″ electric drill to drill nail holes on each side of the I-beam, up through the top plate. Drill these holes in pairs, 16″ o.c. (on center), the complete length of the I-beam. Then drive 16d (penny) nails through the holes so they hold the top plate against the steel I-beam. Then use a carpenter's claw hammer to clinch the tips of the nails where they protrude through the top side of the bottom flanges. Remove the C-clamps. Now you can drop a plumb line from the top plate to the floor, install the bottom or sole plate on the concrete, and toenail the studs between the top and sole plates. Position the studs either 16″-o.c. or 24″-o.c.

Fastening Wood to Concrete

Again, use construction adhesive on any tough fastening job, such as fastening sole plates to concrete floors, or fastening furring strips to concrete block or poured concrete walls.

Although adhesives will do most of the work of bonding the wood to the concrete surface, you should augment the adhesive with either concrete nails or power pins driven by a powder-actuated nailing tool. This is a job that conquers many homeowners, so here are the tricks pros use.

First: Always wear protective goggles when using any tools. This is especially critical when driving nails, especially hardened nails, that may go flying off the hammer head and become deadly projectiles.

Second: *Never, never* use a carpenter's claw hammer for driving other tools or hardened nails. The carpenter's hammer is made for driving and pulling nails in wood. Aside from the fact that you

may damage the head (face) of the hammer if you use it on hardened nails, the carpenter's hammer is the poorest possible tool for the job: it is simply too light to drive nails into concrete. I am constantly amazed to see how-to instructions that show the handyman using a carpenter's hammer on hardened nails. (So is the Hand Tool Institute, which abhors and constantly warns against the practice.) Use a heavier, 2-lb. mash or machinist's hammer for driving concrete nails. The reason so many handymen repeatedly bend concrete nails is that, using the lighter carpenter's hammer, they must strike the concrete nail dozens of blows to try and sink it into the concrete. Most often, the nail bends before it is driven.

Third: Select the proper concrete nail for the job. Round concrete nails are designed to be driven into solid (poured) concrete walls or slabs such as floors. If you try to drive the round nail into concrete block, the nail will simply punch an oversized hole into the hollow core of the block, and there will be no holding power in the nail.

For nailing into concrete block walls, use cut (flat) concrete nails, and drive them into the mortar joints between the blocks, not into the body of the block itself. Like its round cousin, the flat nail will simply punch an oversized hole into the hollow core concrete block, with no holding power on the nail. It should also be noted that the flat nail should be positioned so the long, flat face of the nail is parallel with, not perpendicular to, the furring strip. The mortar joint, being solid concrete, will hold the nail firmly. You should also use the heavier, 2-lb. hammer, when driving cut or flat concrete nails, for the same reason: the face of the heavier hammer is not so likely to chip, and the extra weight is needed to drive the nails into the hard concrete.

Another tip: don't overnail. When fastening furring strips to concrete walls, you can limit the number of nails or driven pins needed by using adhesives. Lay on a heavy bead of adhesive, about

⅜", to bridge over uneven spots in the wall, and to ensure good contact with the very porous concrete surface. Then drive a nail into the top mortar joint, one in the mortar joint closest to the floor, and a third nail into the mortar joint at the center of the wall. These three nails normally provide plenty of holding power, in conjunction with the adhesives. If you drive them properly, and use the right nail, you can get a good connection with fewer fasteners.

Furring

To ensure getting straight furring strips, rip 1 × 2s from wider 1-by material such as 1 × 6, and rip them just when you are ready to install the furring. The narrow furring strips, left out in high humidity storage sheds around lumber yards tend to twist and warp rapidly, and become unusable.

Insulating panels such as Styrofoam® can be used as insulation between furring strips. The insulating foam panels are available in ¾" thickness, so they fit between 1 × 2 furring strips. The foam panels are available either 14½" wide for framing 16" on center (from the center of one framing member to the center of the next) or 22½" wide for framing 24" o.c. (on center).

It is wrong to try to apply all the furring strips first, then fit the foam insulating panels between the furring strips. Because the furring strips usually are neither straight nor uniform in width, the foam panels must be trimmed; the resulting fit is imperfect, and the insulation barrier loses a great deal of its efficiency. The right procedure is to nail/glue a furring strip at the corner of an exterior wall, position a foam panel next to the strip, fasten a second furring strip tight against the edge of the panel, then install another panel, etc. Alternating the installation of furring strips and insulating panels lets you flex the furring strips tight against the foam insulating panels, so the panels present a crack-free barrier to cold infiltration.

One overlooked area to insulate is the band joist area, where the concrete walls meet the framing or band joist. This is the longest continuous crack in the house, because it is uninterrupted for the entire length of the house perimeter. The simplest solution is to caulk the crack between the mud sill (the flat framing member atop the concrete basement walls) and the top block course. When you have caulked the crack, cut fiberglass insulation batts and insert them where the floor joists meet the band joist and mud sill.

When furring is in place, along with the foam insulating panels, use caulk or aerosol foam insulation to seal cracks around ducts or electrical outlets. When you are satisfied with the thoroughness of your insulation job, apply a 4-mil polyethylene vapor barrier over the entire insulated exterior wall area. Overlap the vapor barrier at joints by at least 8" to be sure you have an absolute air and moisture seal.

Framing a 2 × 4 Wall

If the exterior walls are uneven, or if you want added insulation, you may choose to build a new 2 × 4 wall inside the existing exterior basement walls. Using a full 2 × 4 for framing depth of 3½" lets you install batt insulation of fiberglass that is 3½" thick, for an R-factor of 11, compared to about 4½-R for the ¾" thick foam insulation panels.

The easiest way to frame a 2 × 4 wall is to cut the sole and top plates to length, clamp them together, then use a carpenter's square and tape to measure and mark off the stud locations. Secondary 2 × 4 walls for a basement can be built with the 2 × 4s on 24" centers, or with 22½" spacing between the 2 × 4s. This wall will serve as a screen only, and will not bear any loading, so the spacing is not important from a strength standpoint. Nor will you need a double top plate, for the same reason: no strength is needed.

Build 2 × 4 walls on the floor, then tip them up into position. Use construction adhesives and/or concrete nails to secure the sole plate to the concrete floor; drive 16d (penny) nails through the top 2 × 4 plate and into the joists. Use a carpenter's level to plumb the walls. Photo courtesy of Owens/Corning Fiberglas.

Install friction-fit fiberglass batt insulation between the studs on outside walls, or on walls you want to soundproof. The value of the insulation depends on how carefully it is installed: leave no gaps. Note the dust mask on the workman. Photo courtesy of Owens/Corning Fiberglas.

After all wiring, plumbing, heating, and insulation are in place, staple a 4-mil polyethylene plastic vapor barrier over the insulation. Do not tear or snag the vapor barrier; overlap the vapor barrier at least 6″ at any joints. Note mask, goggles on workman. Photo courtesy of Owens/Corning Fiberglas.

An alternative is to install fiberglass batt insulation with kraft-paper vapor barrier attached. Using this type of vapor barrier demands careful installation: any wrinkles or gaps in the vapor barrier will defeat your purposes. It doesn't require a large hole for airborne moisture to pass through. Photo courtesy of Owens/Corning Fiberglas.

An area that is often overlooked when insulating is the band joist area where floor joists meet the concrete basement. Install insulation batts around the entire rim joist area of the house. This is the longest crack in the house, so plug it well. Note long-sleeved shirt, gloves, eye and mask protection, all recommended when working with insulation. Photo courtesy of Owens/Corning Fiberglas.

Install wallboard after the vapor barrier is in place. If the ceiling will be a tiled or suspended ceiling, install wallboard on walls first; if the ceiling is wallboard, then install ceiling first, before walls, so wall panels will cover cracks around ceiling edges. Photo courtesy of Owens/Corning Fiberglas.

When you have laid out the 2 × 4 top and bottom (sole) plates, and marked the 2 × 4 stud locations on both plates, position the 2 × 4 studs between the top and bottom plates. All plates and studs are set on edge, and 16d (penny) nails are driven into the ends of the studs, through the top and bottom plates. Continue nailing until you have secured all the 2 × 4 studs to both top and bottom plates, then grasp the top edge of the framed wall and tilt it upwards into position against the outside wall. Remember, as you build these walls, that your head room or tilt-up height is limited because of the ceiling above. Build the 2 × 4 wall frames so they are slightly shorter than the total ceiling height, or you will be stuck with wall frames that are too tall to tilt up. After you have tilted the wall frames into position, you can drive cedar shingle shims between the top plates of the walls and the bottom edge of the ceiling joists above, and nail the top plate into the bottom of the joists. Secure the bottom or sole plates to the concrete floor with concrete nails or power pins from a driver. You can either augment or substitute the concrete nails with construction adhesive to hold the sole plate to the concrete floor. Plumb the walls with a level.

When you have finished furring or framing all the exterior walls, use the same tilt-up method to frame interior wall partitions. Use a carpenter's level to check the walls for plumb as you proceed. Also, be sure to add backing at ceiling and wall corners.

Framing Door Openings

Interior doors usually are 32 inches wide, but consider using wider doors for easier passage, especially if you have elderly or handicapped family members who find narrow doors limit their access. Consider also using pocket or sliding doors in areas where space is limited, such as bathrooms or storage closets that open onto standard-width (3-foot wide) hallways. Also, consider using bifold or bypass closet doors that not only do not swing into the room, but also permit access to the full width of the closet.

Select pre-hung doors carefully, and bring them home before you frame the door openings. It is very easy to frame the opening to the wrong measurements and have to alter it, if you do not have the door unit handy for ready measuring reference.

When planning for the door opening, measure the actual width of the doorpack: that is, the combined width of the door, plus the ¾″ jambs on both sides of the door. Then allow another inch (1-inch) so that you have ½-inch space on each side of the jambs, in the rough door frame. This ½-inch space is allowed so you can move the door unit from side to side, to plumb and shim the unit in the opening, even if the jackstuds on either side are not straight.

The door frame consists of two studs that reach from the sole or bottom 2 × 4 plate to the bottom side of the top plate, called "king studs." These are installed so the distance between them, figured from the edge of one king stud to the edge of the other king stud (not o.c., or center-to-center) is the width of your rough opening, plus 3″. The 3″ extra space permits you to fit two jack studs, cut 80⅞″ long, inside the two king studs. The jack studs fit atop the sole plate and extend up to the bottom side of the header. The header is a 2 × 4, cut to fit between the two king studs, with their ends atop the jack studs. The header bottom should be set at 82⅜″ from the floor.

You should frame the door opening, leaving the bottom 2 × 4 or sole plate intact. Tilt the wall frame up into position, plumb it, and fasten it to the concrete floor. Note: Do not put nails or adhesive under the sole plate section that sits in the door opening. This section of the sole plate must be cut out after the wall is in place and anchored. Note that if you wish to block sound transfer between two rooms you can use acoustic caulk to seal the cracks between framing members and the floor, ceiling, or other framing members.

Framing Soffits (Drop Ceilings)

Soffits (sometimes called "drop ceilings") are framework placed around ceiling obstructions so they become a level, even surface for finishing. Soffits are framed to cover furnace ductwork, plumbing, pipes, electrical wires, or conduits — anything that breaks up the ceiling plane and presents an obstruction to finishing.

If you visit do-it-yourself finished basements, you will sometimes find soffits that are crooked or out of level and plumb. In many cases, the amateur carpenter tries to build the soffits in place, piece by painful piece. Professionals frame the soffit on the floor, building a box frame, or U-shaped box, large enough to cover the ceiling obstruction. Then the soffit is lifted as one piece, fit over the duct or other obstruction, and the frame is nailed or screwed in place.

The best tool for building the soffits is a power screwgun or wallboard screwgun, with wallboard screws, various shapes of metal connectors, and adhesives. Begin by assembling sufficient 2 × 2s to make the soffit. If headroom is limited, you may prefer to use 1 × 4s, laid flatways, across the bottoms of the soffits.

Measure the length of soffit needed, and lay out top and bottom plates (2 × 2s) this length. If long soffits are needed, say the length of a 20-foot long room, the soffits can be built in two or more sections and lifted into place separately, then aligned and screwed together at the ceiling.

Next, measure the depth of the soffits. If ductwork extends down 12″ below the ceiling, for example, we would want the soffits to be 12″, plus the thickness of a 2 × 2, or 1½″, plus a small allowance for clearance, say another ½″. This means the overall depth of the soffit would be 12″ + 1½″ + ½″ = 14″ total. From this total we subtract 3″, the combined thickness of the top and bottom plates, for a remainder of 11″. Thus the 2 × 2 spacers between the top and bottom plates would be 11″ long. We then mark and cut a number of 2 × 2s, each 11″ long. The total number cut will depend on the distance between the spacer 2 × 2s, which could be 24″.

Laying the top and bottom 2 × 2 plates parallel, and positioning the 11″ long 2 × 2s between them, we fasten all the pieces into a ladder, with the 11″ spacers between the two plates, and fastened to the plates with wallboard screws or, optionally, metal connectors and nails.

If the soffit is to be U-shaped, fitting over the duct or other obstruction, we then build an identical second ladder, or side frame, with an overall width of 14″. Measure the width of the duct, from side to side across the bottom of the duct. This measurement, plus a ½″ allowance for unevenness in the duct, becomes the length of our crosspiece. If 2 × 2s are used for the crosspieces (assuming that headroom isn't critical), we position the 2 × 2s between the bottom plates of the two side frames or ladders, and use 2½″-long wallboard screws to screw the side frames to the ends of the bottom 2 × 2 crosspieces. If headroom is a problem, we might build the side frames or ladders only 12″ wide, so they extend only to the bottom edge of the ducts. We would then use 1 × 4 crosspieces to hold the two sides of the U-shaped soffit in line, and gain about ¾″ in headroom under the finished soffit.

When the framing is assembled, lift the soffit up against the ceiling, over the ducts or obstruction, and use the screwgun to drive 2½″-long wallboard screws through the top 2 × plate, and into the joists above. If the top plate of the soffit does not line up with the joists, i.e., if the plate of the soffit runs parallel to the joists rather than perpendicular to them, you will have to install nailers between the two joists above your soffit. Cut 2 × 4 blocks, usually 14½″ long, to fit between the pair of joists. Position the 2 × 4 blocks between the pair of joists, and 2 or 3 feet apart. Drive 2½″-long wallboard screws through the joists, into the ends of the 2 × 4 blocks, being careful to align the bottom of the

2 × 4 blocks with the bottom edges of the joists. Now you can drive 2½″-long wallboard screws through the top 2 × 2 plates of the soffits, into the cross-blocks you have installed between the joists. As you drive the screws, check frequently with a measuring tape to be sure that the 2 × 2 top plate is straight. Or, chalk a line along the edge of the duct so you will have an alignment mark to guide by when you position the soffit frame in place.

Smaller obstructions, that do not require a soffit to cover them, can be allowed for by nailing furring strips alongside them. For example, if ¾″ water pipes, or electrical conduit, run on the bottom side of the joists, you can just nail 1 × 2 furring strips to the bottom edges of the joists, between the obstructions, then cover them over with wallboard or other ceiling material.

```
┌─────────────────────────────────────┐
│       TOOL LIST FOR INSULATING       │
│   ☐ Razor knife                      │
│   ☐ Straight edge                    │
│   ☐ Staple gun                       │
│   ☐ Staples                          │
│   ☐ Gloves                           │
│   ☐ Face mask                        │
│   ☐ Goggles                          │
│   ☐ Long-sleeve shirt                │
│   ☐ Measuring tape                   │
└─────────────────────────────────────┘
```

INSULATION

In the first part of this chapter we discussed using foam insulation panels (see Furring section). You will find further references to insulation in Chapter 8 in the section on Soundproofing, Fireproofing. Why the scattered references to insulation as a topic? Because there are so many kinds of insulation — foam insulating panels, aerosol foam products, fiberglass or mineral wood batts — that you are forever using insulation in a building project. There are as many or more uses for insulation as there are types of insulation. For example, we talked about the foam insulation panels because they should be installed, alternately, with the furring strips, to ensure a good fit between the panels and the strips. But some insulation should not be placed until all the mechanical work is in place. You can't string electrical wiring, install heating or cold air ducts, or install plumbing without disturbing insulation that is already in place. So, it makes no sense to install the batt insulation, then try to work around it, in exterior walls.

So, in our work sequence, we indicated that insulation should not be installed until the mechanical work is in place. But you'll be advised to use insulation for one or another reason throughout the book, because insulation serves a number of purposes.

The primary purpose of insulation is to prevent or obstruct the flow of heat to cold. One of nature's laws is that heat always flows to cold; and it will flow through any path available to it. I remember when I was an apprentice, the least experienced man on the crew was assigned the task of installing the insulation. Batt insulation can be disagreeable to work with, because the glass fibers will irritate the unknowing. You should always cover your skin, and protect both your eyes and breathing apparatus, when installing fiberglass insulation. So the cry was "let the cub do it." The other point was that everyone believed the "cub" or apprentice *could* do it, because insulating was thought to be about as simple as a job could be. The result is that the great majority of insulation installed before the energy crisis was installed incorrectly, as witness the size of our oil appetites and our heating bills.

Let me point out that insulation tests conducted by Chevron, in the Pacific area that included Portland, Oregon, showed that any void or hole in the insulation could render that insulation almost totally useless. All the "cubs" — and some of us who

Resilient channel can also help soundproof ceilings. Note the channel is nailed perpendicular to the wood joists. Using the channel aids sound control, lets you stagger end (butt) joints while ensuring they will be flat, and provides supports for the batt insulation overhead. Photo courtesy of Owens/Corning Fiberglas.

Detail of resilient channel on ceilings. Note the channel rides over uneven double joists to provide flatter ceiling. Also note the louver-type slots in the sides of the channel. These slots let the channel flex and absorb sound waves for better sound control. Photo courtesy of Owens/Corning Fiberglas.

should have known better — thought that if we covered 90% of a wall, that was good enough. But tests show that a hole in the insulation the *size of your fist* will reduce the effectiveness of the insulation by 40% or more. Why is that true? Because that natural law we mentioned, that heat is always trying to flow to cold, and is always seeking a path to do so, means that in effect the heat loss is occurring as though it was under pressure. Like air pressure in a tire, you don't need a large hole to lose the air. So any little void in the insulation has a great effect on the value of the insulation job.

That "cub" we mentioned was given a screwdriver or paint scraper and told to stuff batt insulation into cracks around window and door jambs. And stuff it he did: he packed that insulation into the cracks until they would hold no more. This "more is better" theory of course ignored the fact that insulation is most effect when it is fluffed up, and becomes less effective as a heat barrier the more it is compressed. Rule one: Leave insulation batts fluffed.

The second rule for batt insulation is: never leave any void in the insulation. Any pro will tell you that building tradesmen who found insulation in the way of an electrical outlet box just tore away a fistful of the batt, rather than cutting and fitting the insulation carefully around the box, or water pipe or whatever was being installed. Those small holes in the insulation barrier are as leaky as a small hole in your car's tire, and thermography will bear this claim out. Rule two: fit insulation with care, because heat is always seeking a path to cold.

Another insulation tip concerns batt insulation that has a kraft-paper or an aluminum-foil vapor barrier attached to the face of the batt. Like insulation, a vapor barrier that has holes, cuts, or gaps in it is no barrier to moisture passage. Examine a construction job where the faced insulation batts have been stapled carelessly in place, with the edge flanges torn, wrinkled, and crooked. Do these gaps between the flanges and the wall framing look wa-

terproof? Vapor barrier means, literally, that you are trying to prevent water, in vapor form, from passing into the wall or ceiling. Rule three: batt insulation that has a foil or kraft facing on it must have the edges fitted together like fine wallcovering. How large a gap would you guess would be needed to allow moisture to sneak through? Avoid wrinkles, tears, or gaps in the vapor barrier face of batt insulation, or they will cause you future trouble in the form of wet insulation, rotted framing or wallboard, and peeled paint on the exterior.

Because of the "avoid any gap" rule in both insulation and vapor barriers, we urge that you inspect the total job before you cover it up. Push — but don't pack — fiberglass insulation into any crack you can find. Caulk any cracks with a latex caulking compound, or use an aerosol foam product, to really seal the insulation airtight. Check, then check again, to make your barrier as complete as possible. Seal any joints or tears in the poly plastic vapor barrier with duct tape. Look for spots that have been overlooked, or where damage has occurred from materials or tools that have been carelessly handled. When you cover the wall or ceiling up, you've lost your opportunity to correct any mistakes.

Insulation as Soundproofing

The job of major soundproofing, stopping sound passage between rooms or between floors in a house, is discussed in Chapter 8, along with wallboard installation. But insulation is also used as soundproofing on smaller applications. Pushing fiberglass insulation in pipe holes through framing will help cushion the pipes from banging due to expansion and contraction. Full-thick insulation placed in plumbing walls, and fitted carefully around any plumbing, will muffle those embarrassing gurgling noises that often flow through bathroom walls. Laundry, workshop, even bedroom walls can be insulated with batts to help eliminate one of the most pervasive forms of pollution: the noise pollution that grows daily in this nation.

7
Plumbing, Heating, and Electrical

TOOL LISTS

Plumbing
- [ ] Pipe wrenches, 2
- [ ] Adjustable wrench pliers, 2 pairs
- [ ] Screwdriver(s)
- [ ] Hacksaw
- [ ] Tubing cutter (for copper or plastic)
- [ ] Measuring tape
- [ ] Hammer
- [ ] Pipe dope, compound or solvent
- [ ] Drill, bits, hole saws
- [ ] Propane torch (copper)
- [ ] Solder

Heating
- [ ] Tin ships
- [ ] Cold chisel
- [ ] Pop rivet tool, assorted rivets
- [ ] Tools from above list, as needed

Electrical
- [ ] Wire-cutting pliers
- [ ] Wire strippers
- [ ] Electrician's tape
- [ ] Tools from above lists, as needed

The mechanical systems of a house — plumbing, heating, and electrical — are the most closely monitored parts of the building job. This is true because the potential exists for errors that could cause loss of life and property: both your own and the community's. As we noted in the beginning of the book, it is important to take out permits for the job, and separate permits as required for the mechanicals. In my own community a job permit is required. The job permit covers all the structural, excavating, interior, and exterior aspects of the house. Also required is a city license for a Heating permit. Unless you are doing the work on your own home, the work must be done by a licensed contractor.

Plumbing and Electrical licenses are available from your local building department in most instances, but the licenses for these contractors are issued by the state. Some states and cities are very tough about this licensing/permit procedure; the rule in the past has been to prohibit or discourage the homeowner from doing his own work. In some cities where trade unions are strong, political pressures worked against letting non-union or unlicensed persons do any of the mechanical trades. As the do-it-yourself industry has expanded, materials are increasingly easy to work with, so we do not need the expensive tools that were required in the past. I remember, for example, when huge threading dies were hauled into the house to thread galvanized water pipe: in those days it took a plumber up to a full week just to cut, thread, and install the piping for a house. This gave way to using copper supply pipes, and two plumbers would often start piping a house in the morning and be gone by noon, with all the pipe roughed in. Today, slip-lock connectors and plastic pipe have reduced the chore of plumbing to a few hours' work, and a few hand tools.

By the same token, many jurisdictions required the use of greenfield (flexible steel cable) or conduit for wiring. One of these tubings was installed, and the electrician pulled a black (hot) and white (neutral) wire into each receptacle with a tool called a snake. The ground was provided by the cable or conduit, which was continuous back to the entry box. Today, house wiring is usually done with Romex™, a three-wire plastic cable that combines three wires: hot, neutral, and ground (ground wire is either bare copper or has green insulation). The outlet boxes or receptacles are also of plastic, with the continuous ground being the green or bare copper wire.

Should you attempt your own mechanical work, or part of it? The best advice is: maybe. It depends on how experienced you are, how extensive the job is, permit requirements in your area, and also area wage scales. In areas where trade wages are low-to-middle range, it may not be a paying proposition, from a financial standpoint, to do your own work. If you are even a little wary of your own ability to do it right, hire the work done and save your money someplace else. I'll attempt to give you some guidance that will help you decide whether the jobs are within your scope.

PLUMBING

Plastic supply pipe can be cut with a handsaw, with a razor knife, or even a pair of tin snips (depending on the type of pipe or tubing). You can buy snap-together fixtures such as couplings to join the pipes together. Shutoff valves may require using two wrenches or adjustable pliers, to turn the nuts on the valves and make them watertight. There are snap-on or twist-on plastic connectors for installing new lines from existing copper or galvanized supply pipes. Keep in mind that it has been some years since galvanized pipe use was common, and if you are finishing your basement, it might be an opportune time to repipe your house, before you cover old pipes up. One problem with galvanized pipe was that it tended to let minerals build up on the inside of the pipe and eventually to plug the pipes completely, making replacement necessary. Copper and plastic are much less likely to plug up.

If you are piping in water supply pipes to a bathroom, that is well within most people's ability. If you have wet bars, kitchen, bathroom with exotic whirlpool plumbing and extra water heaters, think it over.

Installing New Drain Pipes

Installing drains once meant working with a 3″ or 4″ diameter cast-iron pipe, and having the tools for cutting and assembling it. One of the necessary tools was a lead pot: the end of one pipe was inserted into the bell housing on the next pipe, the pipe joint was packed tight with plumber's oakum (a tar-soaked rope used to get tight joints in plumbing or boat construction) and lead was melted and poured into the joint over the oakum. The lead fumes in those old houses would clear your sinuses, and affect you in other strange ways.

Today, most cities will let you use plastic drain pipe. Where cast-iron is still used, you can connect the pipe together using connectors that look like the clamps on your car's radiator hoses. The pipes are now made without the bell housing or hubs; the system and the connectors are called "no-hub." The connectors have a stainless steel metal band with screw tighteners like the radiator clamps men-

MINIMUM FIXTURE SPACING FOR BATHROOMS

Distance, inches	From fixture	To fixture or wall
16″	Stool, C.L.*	Wall (side) Sink (near edge) Tub (near end)
12″	Stool, C.L.	Back wall (finished)
20″	Lavatory, C.L. (sink)	Wall (side)
15″	Lavatory, edge	Stool, C.L.
16″	Tub, edge	Stool, C.L.
24″	Tub, edge Lavatory, front	Stool, front Stool, front
30″	Tub, edge	Lavatory, front

NOTE: Distances listed between fixtures or fixtures and walls are minimum distances. If space permits, or you have family members who lack good mobility, increase distances.

*C.L. where listed means "center line."

tioned. Riveted to the stainless steel band is a neoprene sleeve that has a ridge on the inside, at the middle. Just slip the no-hub connector over the pipe until the end of one pipe is tight against that ridge, which seals the crack between the two pipe ends so they won't leak. Then slip the second pipe into the open end until it too butts against the sealing ridge in the center of the connector. Use a wrench or large screwdriver to tighten the retaining screws until everything is snug.

The worst problem of working with drain pipes today is breaking out the concrete floor to make the connection to the existing drain. A large sledge hammer, 8-lb. or so, can be used to break out the concrete. Starting the hole in the concrete is tough; once you break through the floor slab, you can break away a trench by just hitting the edge of the

hole you have opened, chipping away the concrete. The floor slab is rarely more than 4″ thick, and may break fairly easily. Or, you may need to use a masonry chisel to help break away the slab.

Finding the existing drain pipes, and main drain, is fairly simple. Look around the basement floor for floor drains, drains for the laundry tubs or clothes washer, existing toilet drain, and where the main drain exits the house to the street sewer. When you have located these existing drains, you can determine where the drain pipes run under the floor slab by drawing an imaginary line (or snap a chalkline) between the floor drain and drain exit, or the toilet drain and drain exit.

After breaking out the concrete and exposing the drain pipe, you must cut a section of the old pipe away so you can make your connection. Depending on your particular project, and how the new drain will meet the existing drain pipe, you will need either a T-fitting or a Y-fitting (so named for the shape of the fittings) to connect between the old and new drain pipes. If you make a rough drawing of your floor plan and how the drain pipes come together, your plumbing supply man can help you select the right pieces for assembly. Once you have the pieces together, you can join them with no-hub connectors. Then, after inspection, mix some concrete and refill, level and finish the concrete in the trench or hole you have cut.

Drain Vents

There is no such thing as an empty drain pipe: if the pipe is not full of water, it is full of air. That is why you must provide vents on drain lines, so the air can flow out as water flows in. Added fixture drains can piggyback the existing vents, providing the new fixture is within specified distances from the vented drain line. These distance limits are:

> For 2″ drain, 5′
> For 3″ drain, 6′
> For 4″ drain, 10′, to the vented drain line.

If drains are added for toilet stool, shower, bathtub, or lavatory, they must be within the above distance limits if the vents are to work properly. Fixtures added beyond these limits must have new vents. Lack of proper venting can cause drains to back up, or to be noisy. If you have drains that make gurgling noises when water is running through them, this indicates that the vents do not supply enough air, so a bit of water is running out, air rushes in, a bit more water runs out, etc., with a "gulp" noise at each stage of the cycle. Drains that are properly vented let the water flow out quickly and quietly.

HEATING

In most cases your existing furnace will be large enough to heat your new space also. Installing new ducts for the space still requires that you run ducts to each separate room, to ensure that you have sufficient heat circulation. You can use the cavities between two wall studs as a cold air return channel; just install a mount between the two to hold the register cover.

Often, with forced-air systems, there are registers cut into the basement side of the duct that services the room(s) above. If you live in a cold climate you may not want to try bleeding the heat (or air-conditioning) off the upstairs ducts. Keep in mind that forced air won't easily change direction: if you blow it straight down a supply duct, it will not turn a corner and flow with any amount of force downward to the space below, in the basement. It is best to install new room ducts to each room, to ensure there is plenty of heat in cold weather.

If you have hot water heat, have a contractor install a new hot water supply loop into the area to be finished. In newer houses, where finishing the basement was anticipated, contractors normally have already installed at least some baseboard radiator units.

Auxiliary Heating

If your basement is normally quite warm in winter, and you will use a basement recreation room only for occasional parties, you may want to install auxiliary heaters. Modern heaters are available for just such purposes; they could almost be called portable heaters because of their versatility. Some options that are inexpensive and are well-suited for occasional use include the electric baseboard heaters. These have built-in or wall thermostats, can be easily installed by just running a 220V electrical supply to the site, and offer quick heat-up for temporary use.

Fireplaces fall into the auxiliary heating class. You would not ordinarily want to have a fireplace running continuously, whether the fireplace is wood or gas fired. But modern free-standing fireplaces offer random installation, because no massive chimney is needed. Steel chimneys can be run out the side of the basement wall and up the house to the rooftop. The chimney can then be enclosed with plywood and the plywood can be covered over with man-made stone, lightweight featherstone (a volcanic product) or a veneer brick, so they approximate the massive appearance of a full masonry fireplace.

Can you install these fireplaces yourself? The first story I wrote as a how-to magazine editor was how to install your own fireplace. Freestanding fireplaces have been improved since those days, back in the old energy crunch. The fireplaces are now available with fresh air ducts to bring in combustion air; they have fan units for better heat circulation; in gas models you can have wall-mounted thermostats and remote ignition devices. And, the range of styles and sizes offered has grown, too: 42″ models are now available for "great room" applications.

ELECTRICAL

This is another area where I urge you to consider the scope of the job, plus your own experience, before you decide to tackle the job yourself. Installing electrical circuits for outlets is not too tricky. But other considerations, such as lighting, wiring power to water heaters, whirlpool tubs, or baseboard electric heating units, may take you into territory where you don't feel comfortable.

But, like the other mechanical trades, manufacturers have been busy trying to make life easy for the homeowner. The first item, of course, is the wiring itself. Romex™ is safe, inexpensive, and approved for most wiring applications. (You must still use conduit to conceal wires that run down concrete walls, or would otherwise be exposed to damage, if you don't finish the wall.) Romex™ is available in various sizes, with 14 gauge being approved for lighting or receptacle wiring. Check local code to see what size wire you require, or check the library for the latest edition of the National Electrical Code book for the code requirements for any part of your job.

Romex™ also has the advantage of go-anywhere flexibility, so you can turn corners or go around obstructions with an ease unknown in the old conduit days. Just bore holes in the studs or joists and string the Romex™ to an outlet location. You can buy a wire stripper to strip off the wire insulation, and this is a must-have. You should not use a knife to strip the plastic insulation from the wires, because you might nick the wire and cause it to break.

Aside from the wire, switches and receptacles are also improved. Older wiring devices had side-mounted screws for attaching the wires. Modern devices also have the screws, but offer the alternative of push-in, pin-release wire connection. You just strip the insulation off the end of the wire (back about ½″: there is a stripping gauge on the back of the device) and push the wire into the retaining hole in the back. Pull gently but firmly on all wires, whether screw attached or inserted in the retaining hole, to be sure the wire is firmly held and will not come loose or cause an arc between the loose wire and the device.

Gas wall heater can be fired as auxiliary heater to take the chill off basement rooms. The unit has a direct vent, eliminates need for a chimney pipe. Viewing area of glass door is 15" × 27"; gas logs give the look of a wood-burning fireplace. Unit can be hung on wall or supported on a pedestal; 70 percent energy efficiency rating with 21,000 input BTU makes unit highly effective. Optional fan helps heat circulation; approved for use with a wall thermostat. Photo courtesy of Heat-N-Glo Fireplace Products Inc.

Oasis model is so named because it can be installed as a four-sided fireplace unit; lets you install the unit anyplace where you can position an 8" metal chimney. For wood-burning and gas logs. Photo courtesy of Heat-N-Glo Fireplace Products Inc.

If you have a fireplace that extends out into the room, and you don't know what to do about it, take a look at this solution by Designer Margot Gunther, ASID. Ms. Gunther executed this treatment to resemble an English country sitting room. Enclosed in wood paneling, the fireplace opening has a marble face and brass screen and utensils. Storage cabinets at each end hold books or home entertainment equipment; they could easily be wood boxes if needed. Photo courtesy of Plywood Paneling Council.

OWNER'S INSPECTION CHECKLIST — PLUMBING

NOTES

_____ Water heater is set and hooked up.

_____ Main water shut-off valve is in place, easily accessible, and works properly.

✓ Water faucets on all water supply pipes: hot water is on the left, cold water is on the right.

✓ Check faucets at tub, vanity, laundry to be sure faucets are working and are not restricted.

✓ Check water pressure and volume flow by turning on all faucets and flushing toilet simultaneously. Only minimum drop in water flow should be noted.

_____ Run clothes washer through wash cycle. Check for leaks and water hammer noises in water supply pipes.

_____ Check tub, shower stall, toilet, and ceramic tile for any chipping or damage to the finishes.

✓ Turn all faucets on and off quickly and listen for water hammer or vibration noises in pipes.

✓ Check all drains for water flow. Run showers and tubs with faucets wide open.

_____ If you haven't already done so, have a professional clean all drains, including the main drain all the way to the sewer at the street.   _CALLED BROWN 555-1821_

✓ Run water down each branch drain and listen for bubbling or gurgling noises that indicate insufficient venting.

_____ If extra roof vents for plumbing have been installed, check the roof for proper vent flashing.

_____ In stocking feet, stand in new tubs or showers to be sure they are firmly in place and tub or shower base does not move or rock. Check also for a "kerplunk" noise in fiberglass shower base as you step into or out of the shower. Any noise indicates a poor-quality base that flexes with a person's weight: the thin base will soon crack from flexing, leaving you with an expensive problem — a leaking base.

✓ Call for final plumbing inspection. An experienced inspector may catch code violations that can be corrected before they cause you problems and added expense.   _555-0181_

OWNER'S INSPECTION CHECKLIST — ELECTRICAL

✓ Electrical outlets per code, no more than 12 ft. apart. Switches black (power) wire only.

✓ Outlet boxes are positioned so front edge of box is flush with wallboard or paneling.

✓ Room circuits are 15 amp; laundry room circuits per equipment needs.

✓ All bath, laundry circuits have ground fault circuit interrupters for wet shock protection.

✓ All circuits are grounded. Check to be sure system grounding has not been interrupted due to plumbing or other changes.

____ Bath ventilator fans are installed and working properly.

____ Dimmer switches installed as per specifications.

✓ Furnace and central air are operational.

✓ No scratches or damage to new appliances: check laundry, furnace and dehumidifier.Security system, smoke alarms are installed and working.

✓ All lighting is in place, fixtures attached, switches working.

____ Intercom, radio, phones are connected and working.

____ Hot tubs, whirlpool baths are installed and working. CAUTION: Switches should not be within reach of the tub.

✓ Circuit tester or voltmeter shows 117 volts at outlets and fixtures. Check between ground and each socket.

____ Central vacuum cleaner has been installed and is operational.

____ Check recessed light fixtures for recommended bulb size. Oversize bulbs generate too much heat for recessed lighting safety. Use only recommended bulb sizes.

✓ 3 or 4-way switches are installed and work from every location.

✓ Electrical wiring that runs across unfinished (concrete) wall is enclosed in thinwall conduit for protection.

✓ Outlet covers are in place on all outlets and switches.

____ Final inspection has been completed and signed off by inspector.

✓ Warranties on all equipment and appliances have been filed away for future reference.

NOTES

GET 2ND SMOKE ALARM

CHECK SWITCH IN CLOSET

555-0181

8
Working with Wallboard

TOOL LIST

☐ Razor knife, blades
☐ Measuring tape, 12-ft.
☐ Carpenter's pencil, crayon
☐ Nail bag or apron
☐ Wallboard screwgun
☐ Keyhole saw and/or saber saw
☐ Wallboard T-square
☐ Wallboard hammer
☐ Carpenter's square
☐ Chalk line
☐ Wallboard lifter or prybar
☐ Tin snips
☐ Wallboard saw (8 point)
☐ Sawhorses
☐ Scaffold plank, 2 × 12, ten ft. long
☐ Nuisance dust masks
☐ Eye goggles

The first consideration is whether you will do the wallboard work yourself or have it done. A major criticism of how-to writers is their tendency to exaggerate the dollar savings of doing a job yourself.

Installing and finishing wallboard is an example of one area of remodeling that is essentially a job for two people, and should not be undertaken if you do not have helpers you can call on. It is also a good example of an area where the work is difficult for amateurs to perform, and where the cost of professional help is not great.

To decide whether you will do your own wallboard work, call in professionals and ask for bids. If you feel you must do part of the work yourself, have the wallboard installed and do the finishing and painting yourself. In many cases you will find that doing your own wallboard work does not make good economic sense, because the savings are not that great if you subtract the cost of the materials and consider only the labor charges.

DRAWBACKS

What are the drawbacks to doing your own wallboard work? First, it takes two sturdy individuals to haul the heavy wallboard downstairs, heft it for cutting and fitting, then lift it overhead for ceiling installation. The advice, often seen, to use T-props to hold the wallboard panels up is poor advice: if you have a free hand to place the props you may as well use that hand to do what the pros do: nail or screw the panel in place rather than fool around with props. An additional problem, one that is potentially dangerous, is that the props may slip, letting the heavy wallboard panel come crashing down on your head. Always have help when you are installing wallboard on ceilings; never try to do it alone.

Another poor tactic that is often used to make wallboard installation easier for one person is to use smaller 4′ × 8′ panels that are easier to lift. Because the quality of the wallboard project depends on using as large panels as possible to minimize the number of joints that must be finished, using the small 4′ × 8′ panels is poor policy. If possible, use 4′ × 12′ panels to eliminate butt or end joints, and to reduce the total footage of joints that must be treated and concealed. Use 4′ × 8′ panels *only* if access is limited and you can't get the longer panels down the basement stairs.

Keep in mind that the concern is not the weight of the wallboard alone; in addition to being heavy, the large panels are clumsy and are easily damaged. The final argument is that most how-to texts give installation advice as though the main concern was simply to cover up the framing. In fact, you are trying to build an interior surface that will be smooth and attractive. Even more important, you may want to build fireproofing, soundproofing, and resistance to moisture or water damage into the walls and/or ceilings. You must understand something more than how to cut and nail wallboard to make the wall/ceiling perform these functions, in addition to serving as a screen to divide one space from another.

If you are not discouraged from doing the wallboard work yourself, or if your brother-in-law did his own attic and assures you that not only will he be on hand to hold up one end of the panels, but that he found the experience of working with wallboard comparable to a day at the beach, then consider the following do-it-yourself advice, which I

guarantee will ease the task and provide superior results

INSTALLING WALLBOARD

Most texts will observe that you can install wallboard either perpendicular to the framing or parallel to the framing. But all major manufacturers, and the Gypsum Association, agree: the best job results when wallboard is installed perpendicular to the framing. That means that all walls should be installed with 4′ × 12′ panels laid horizontally, not with 4′ × 8′ panels standing up parallel to the wall studs.

The reasons for this are many. You will reduce the total footage of joints to be treated by at least 25% if you install the panels perpendicular to the framing. The joints will be less noticeable, because the joints are positioned so they are not at eye level. (By contrast, all joints parallel to the wall studs are at eye level, no matter what your eye level is, because they are continuous from floor to ceiling.) You can also plan joint placement better when panels are installed perpendicular to the framing. Panels that are "stood up" or installed parallel to the studs make it impossible to avoid having joints at the corners of doors and/or windows. Joints that occur at any point where framing joins together, such as at the corners of door/window headers, will crack when the header lumber shrinks in one direction and the jack studs shrink in the opposite direction. Joints that occur at the corners over window or door headers also interfere with trimming the openings. The tape and compound used to cover the joints make a bulge in the wall right at the point where you are trying to fit a miter joint.

In addition, standing wallboard panels parallel to the wall studs increases a problem called "joint flash" or banding. This is a decorating phenomenon that results when sidelight shines down a wall or ceiling surface. The sidelight magnifies the difference in paint sheen that occurs where the taping compound used to treat the joints meets the face paper of the wallboard panel. There is a difference in suction or porosity between the compound and the paper covering on the wallboard, and you must be sure that wallboard joints are parallel to the light source to minimize this annoying texture difference in the finish paint on wallboard.

The final argument for installing wallboard perpendicular to the framing is that the joints will be flatter and will occur at a comfortable (4-foot) working height on the wall, rather than making you do the monkey-on-a-stick routine of jumping up, then bending over, to finish floor-to-ceiling joints.

Now, plan your wallboard installation. Use a straightedge, at least 6 feet long, to check the framing alignment. Because carpenters install floor joists "crown edge up," the overhead joists to which you will attach your ceiling may be uneven. Use wallboard panel adhesive to help bridge minor framing irregularities. Use a saw to trim any floor joist bridging that protrudes below the level of the joists, because these protrusions can be a real problem if you apply wallboard over them. In addition, mark any high joists — those that arch upwards so their lower edge is higher than the lower edge of adjoining joists — and shim them so they align with the other joists. You can cut ¼"-thick plywood or paneling into 1½"-wide strips and use them for shims to be nailed to the bottom of high joists or on the edge of misaligned wall studs to straighten up ceilings or walls. Continue with the straightedge, checking the alignment of all wall and ceiling framing, before you begin the actual installation. Because wallboard is uniform in thickness it cannot compensate for uneven walls or ceilings as wet plaster can; the finished surface is only as straight as the framing you fasten it to.

As stated, use wallboard adhesives to install wallboard. Of course, you cannot use the adhesives on walls that are covered with plastic vapor barriers, because the adhesive will not stick to the plastic.

Use fasteners (wallboard screws) only on walls or ceilings where you have a plastic vapor barrier.

Adhesives offer many pluses that offset any additional cost. They speed installation of the wallboard because they reduce the number of screws needed. Because there are fewer screws to cover, they speed the finishing steps. Plus, any reduction in screws (or nails) means there are simply that many fewer fasteners to fail or "pop." Also, adhesives can be used where you cannot drive a screw or nail, such as over steel I-beams or on concrete surfaces. Adhesives also should be used where you have wood that is difficult to drive nails or screws into, such as the 1 × 4s on pocket (sliding) doors, or on lightweight soffit lumber.

Nails vs. Screws

In any technology, techniques become obsolete in time when overtaken by better methods. This is true of wallboard construction. One of the primary problems with wallboard in the early days was fastener failure or "nail pops." When screwguns became widely available, and wallboard screws were developed, wallboard application by nailing should have ended, but most texts still show nailing as an acceptable fastening method.

By all means, buy, rent, or borrow a wallboard screwgun if you are finishing a major area such as a basement. Consumer models are available for about $50 in home centers: Sears has a new cordless model. Why the insistence on using a screwgun? First, the degree of fastener "pop" is proportionate to the length of the fastener used. Because screws have better holding power than nails, you can use shorter screws than you would use nails to attach the wallboard: 1"-long screws vs. 1¼"-long nails. So you will have fewer "pops" with screws than with nails. But a better argument for screws is the fact that screwguns can be set so the screws are driven just below the surface of the wallboard.

In contrast, nails are pounded into the wallboard

with a hammer, known in the trades as an "impact tool." This simply means the nail is driven by impact, but the hammer head hits the wallboard with impact, too. From this impact, damage may occur to the face of the wallboard: paper fractures or cuts, nailheads driven until they puncture the paper, and, if the hammer misses the nail, holes driven completely through the wallboard. All of these blemishes make the wallboard more difficult to finish. If the stud or joist is soft and the nail is whacked home, the hammer head may crush the plaster core of the wallboard that surrounds the nail. The crushed plaster will not support the nail, holding power is reduced, and the wallboard panel is loose from the framing, a failure that may become evident only after the surface is painted and the furniture is moved into place. All these problems are eliminated by using screws to attach the wallboard. One final argument for screws is that driving nails into old framing lumber, such as the existing floor joists, is difficult; screws will eliminate all those bent nails from trying to drive small nails into old, dry lumber.

CORNER BLOCKING

When two walls meet, or a wall meets a ceiling, you must provide intermediate blockers or framing to fasten the corners or ends of the wallboard. Installing blocking at corners is usually done during framing. Check all corners for blocking to be sure there is something to screw the wallboard to. If you find it difficult to install wood blocking, as you may where the ceiling joists meet the walls beneath, use adhesive and clamps to attach the wood blocking in the areas where you haven't room to drive a nail or fit a screwgun. Also available are two-way metal corner clips that simply slip over the edges/ends of the adjoining wallboard panels and lock them together. Pick up a few of these metal corner clips at your home center. They will come in handy if you meet a point where there is no corner blocking during the installation. The

clips are available from Gold Bond Building Products under the name Prest-On.

BUTT JOINTS

When you install wallboard perpendicular to the framing you will have joints where two panels butt end to end. Many people point out that these end joints, where two cut ends meet with no recessed edge, are difficult to finish. Here again, it's all in knowing how: pros don't give butt joints a second thought. If you plan these butt joints carefully, so they occur on a joist or stud that is "high" or slightly recessed when compared to the framing member on either side, you can create a slight depression so that end joints finish as flat as edge joints with recessed edges.

First, pick the stud or joist where the butt joint will occur. You are not limited to any one location: place a straightedge over the proposed location, and observe how the straightedge sits on the framing member in relation to the one on either side of it. Let us assume that we are picking a butt joint location on a ceiling. Straightedge the joist you choose plus the ones on either side of it. The straightedge should sit flat on the three joists. If the center joist is much lower than its mates on either side of it, try another location, because the butt joint will be crowned down, lower than its mates, and will thus form a bump or high joint when you fasten the ends of the wallboard panels to it. If all three joists are flat, and the straightedge does not rock when wiggled over the center joist, it can be finished with only a slight crown or bulge over the joint. Keep in mind that when the joist is protruding outward farther than the joists on either side, adding tape and taping compound can only increase the bulge or hump at the center of the joint.

The perfect butt joint location is one where you place a straightedge over the joint location, plus the two joists on either side. While holding the straightedge on this location, look at the center joist. If it is a good candidate for a butt joint location, you will be able to see space or "daylight" under the center of the straightedge. Then, when you screw the panel ends to this joist, it will form a slightly concave joint; when tape and compound are applied over the joint it will be filled so it is flat. Do not place a joint at any location where the framing is not flat, or cannot be filled flat by troweling on taping compound.

Another pro tactic is to check joists or studs and find three that are perfectly aligned, so any joint that occurs on the center joist or stud will be flat. Now apply a ⅜"-thick bead of wallboard adhesive to the joists or studs on either side, but *not* on the center joist or stud. Now screw the panels in place, but apply screws only in the edges of the panel, not in the field, on the framing on either side of the joint. Screw the wallboard at the ends as usual. Now you have "shimmed" (with adhesive) the joists on either side of the joint so the joint is slightly concave; adding tape and compound will make it flat.

The goal is to make your framing as straight as possible, so the butt joints are no worse than level. Measure out from one corner on the wall or ceiling, and choose the joist nearest the end of the wallboard panel as your joint location. Now use the straightedge to see if that joist or stud is level: if it is not, measure out from the opposite corner, or even plan to have *two* butt joints that are flat, rather than having only one butt joint but having that one joint impossible to finish. If possible, plan to have the butt joint fall in the *middle,* not at the corners, of a header over a door or window.

Two things are important when finishing the butt joints. Avoid any heavy build-up of taping compound over the center or apex of the joint, because the more material you pile over the center of the butt joint the more pronounced the bulge at the joint (this is true of finishing *any* joint — the goal is simply to make the joint flat). The second rule to remember is that, by troweling the compound out wide, you can "flare" the butt joint, so the

bulge at the joint is a gradual one, not a sudden pronounced break in the plane.

INSTALLING WALLBOARD CEILINGS

Before installing wallboard ceilings, use a pencil or carpenter's crayon to mark the joist locations on the double top plate of the walls. Put a mark at the center of each joist; bright crayon will show up better. This step will save the tiresome work of holding a wallboard panel against the ceiling while trying to determine just where the joists are. A very basic "secret" of the pros is: don't get the weight of a wallboard panel over — or on — your head, then waste time looking for the framing so you can fasten the panel and turn it loose. You want to swing the panel quickly overhead, position it, check to make sure any cutouts such as ceiling light fixtures are cut to fit, then put a few nails into the panel so you can release it.

Another common mistake for amateurs who install their own wallboard is the failure to build proper scaffold. The proper scaffold or platform for installing wallboard is one that is just tall enough so the installer, holding the wallboard panel atop his head, is just touching the bottoms of the ceiling joists. Trying to work off ladders, or makeshift scaffold, puts the installer in the position of either constantly bending (if the scaffold is too tall) or stretching (if the scaffold is too short). Either position will have you taking a rest break after each panel is installed, because supporting weight while bending or stretching increases fatigue. You will work most efficiently if you are standing erect while installing ceilings.

When fitting and measuring wallboard panels, you should cut the panels slightly shorter than friction-fit, to allow for irregularities in the framing. Let us assume you are installing wallboard in a room that is 12' long, and you are using 12' long wallboard panels. Take two length measurements, one at each edge of the panel location. This will provide a guide as to whether the room is square, or if one

Use a wallboard T-square to make straight cuts across wallboard width. Use a razor knife and replace the blades frequently to avoid tearing the face paper of the wallboard. Photo courtesy of Gold Bond Building Products.

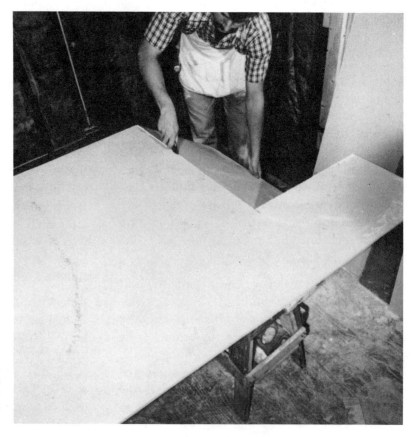

To make a notched cut, saw along the short mark with a wallboard (coarse-tooth) saw, then cut along the long mark with a razor knife. Photo courtesy of Gold Bond Building Products.

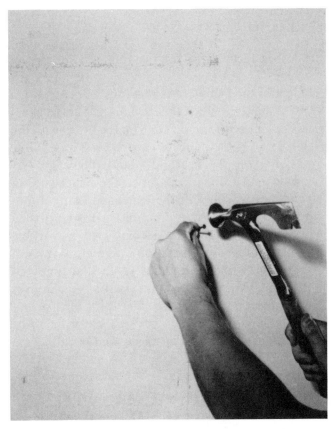

Use special wallboard hatchet for nailing wallboard. The large convex head lets you dimple the wallboard and set the nail slightly without cutting the face paper on the wallboard, as a carpenter's hammer does. The angled handle lets you drive nails without hitting wallboard with your knuckles. Photo courtesy of Gold Bond Building Products.

Preferred method of fastening wallboard is to use a drywall (wallboard) screw gun and wallboard screws. Screw attachment assures wallboard is pulled tight to framing without damaging wallboard. Using screws also means fewer fasteners used, fewer fastener pops. Photo courtesy of Gold Bond Building Products.

or more walls are out of square. If both edge measurements are the same, subtract ½″ from the measurement. For example, if the room is 141″ long, measuring actual length from the top plate of one wall to the top plate of another, subtract ½″ from 141″ and cut the wallboard panel 140½″ long. When you lift the panel into place you thus will have a little "play" between the ends of the panel and the top plates of the walls. Split the difference, so that there is ¼″ gap on each end, not a full ½″ gap at one end and none at the other.

Using this fitting method will eliminate the cut-and-trim procedure that is sure to result if you try to cut the panels absolutely to fit, with no allowance for slight misalignments in the framing. Keep in mind that, if you split the difference so there is ¼″ gap at each end, the wall panels, being ½″ thick, will cover these end gaps. If the room has a butt joint, measure and cut the first panel to meet the center of the joist or stud it will break or occur on. Then measure from the end of the first panel to the top plate at the end wall and subtract only ¼″, because you cannot split this measurement and you don't want more than ¼″ of gap at any end. Remember that you should never force the panel edges together, because you may buckle the panels. Instead, fit the ends and edges of the panels loosely together, just touching but never bowed or forced into position.

I recommend that you use screws to attach the wallboard, for reasons already mentioned. But you may find it an advantage to use a wallboard hammer and nail bag to make the initial attachment of the wallboard to the framing. The procedure is to drive a few nails — a dozen nails at the edges of the panel, and a couple of nails in the center or field of the panel, will hold up the panel while you finish applying screws all over the panel at recommended intervals. This last trick is one often used by pros, who will tack the panels in position with just enough nails to prevent the panels from falling, then come back later and drive screws in a separate operation.

The best procedure for installing wallboard on ceilings is to use two sawhorses, built to fit the height of the installers as previously noted, with a 2 × 12 plank between the sawhorses. Set the panel next to the scaffold, on edge on the floor, with the finish side of the panel toward the workers. While standing on the scaffold plank, both workers should reach down and grasp the panel and, in perfection unison, lift the panel and swing it into position against the ceiling joists. It is surprising how often workers who are not used to working with each other will wind up on opposite sides of the panel, with the obvious result that time and effort are wasted while they reposition themselves so they can work as a team. One thing I can promise: wallboard is heavy, and you will want to be organized so you are not lifting and installing every panel twice.

INSTALLING WALLBOARD WALLS

If the floors are bare, and they should be if you have followed orderly procedure, mark the stud locations on the floor with a carpenter's pencil. Also, mark the locations of heat ducts and electrical outlets on the floor, so if you inadvertently cover over anything you will know just where to find it. The best course is to measure and cut all pipes, outlets, and ducts before installing the wallboard. You should always install wallboard panels so they are perpendicular to the framing; and you should always install the top wall panel first, to cover the edge cracks around the wallboard ceiling, then install the bottom wall panel last. Wallboard lifters are available for lifting the bottom panel in place against the top panel, or you can use a prybar and a block of wood as a fulcrum to lever the panels into position.

As noted, I recommend using wallboard panel adhesives to eliminate 50% — or more — of the fasteners. Some manufacturers state that you need no field screws or nails when you use their adhesives. Just use fasteners on the edges of the panels, where the joint tape will cover and conceal the fasteners. Always apply edge fasteners close to the panel edge: ⅜″ from the edge is recommended.

Adhesives are especially useful when applying wallboard over pocket doors or on soffits, where 1 × 4 boards are often used as space savers. Trying to drive nails into the flat or wide edge of 1 × 4 lumber results in a lumber bounce that pops the nail heads through the wallboard. When driving screws into pocket door frames, use 1″ long screws. Longer screws may penetrate through the wallboard and the 1 × 4 framing, then the screw tips will scratch the door when it is opened.

One common mistake is to drive too many nails or screws around window and door openings. Drive fasteners sparingly around openings, because the finish trim will hold the wallboard in place at the edges. Drive any fasteners as close as possible to the edge of the opening, so the trim will cover fasteners completely. Nails or screws that fall near the edge, but are outside the area covered by finish trim pieces, usually pop when the trim is nailed in place.

When applying wallboard at outside corners, cut the wallboard ends so they are smooth. This way, the steel corner beads used to cover and finish the outside corners will sit straight on the corner and will be easier to finish. One tip is to nail a piece of wire lath or screen over a scrap of 2 × 4. Move this block over the cut ends of the wallboard panels to smooth them for final fitting of the steel corner bead. Nail or screw the corner bead in place, with nails or screws positioned about 6″ apart and in pairs, directly opposite each other. You can cut corner bead where necessary by cutting through the side flanges with a pair of tin snips.

When you are measuring for electrical outlets, make your measurement from the bottom edge of the top wallboard panel, down to the outlet box. Do not measure from the floor upwards to the outlet box. Keep in mind that in most cases you will be lifting the bottom panel up to meet the bottom edge of the top panel, so lifting the bottom panel will change the measurement.

Do not use ordinary wallboard in areas that will be subject to direct moisture contact or high humidity. WR (for water resistant) wallboard, sometimes called "green board" because the face material has a green tinge, is best for walls where high humidity is present, such as the laundry area. WR or "green board" is not recommended for overhead or ceiling installation, because the waterproofing material used in the core plaster makes the green board soft and prone to sagging. Use ordinary wallboard for ceiling applications.

For use as a tile base, buy Durock®, a cement-base material that is made by United States Gypsum as a substrate or base for ceramic tile application. The cement panels, reinforced with fiberglass, are unaffected by direct water contact. Ordinary wallboard will soak or "wick up" any water from leaks in the tub or shower area. When the core of the wallboard gets wet it loses its binder, or becomes soft and chalk-like, and will crumble and destroy the tile surface. Durock® can be sawed, nailed, and cut with a utility or razor knife, so application is no more difficult than wallboard application.

Be very careful when applying Durock® or wallboard in areas where plumbing pipes or electrical wiring run through holes in the wall studs. Nails or screws that are carelessly driven into the wires or pipes can cause water leaks or electrical shorts or fires. Buy flat metal plates and install them on the framing, over wire or pipe locations. The protective plates will help avoid damage to wiring or plumbing from misplaced fasteners. The plates are available at home center stores in the metal connector area with joist hangers and the like.

SOUNDPROOFING, FIREPROOFING

Most walls or ceilings are designed to be privacy curtains between two living areas. Keep in mind that walls or ceilings can be designed to perform

For better sound control, nail resilient steel channel to the wall framing as shown. Install the channel 16" or 24" on center, horizontally, and use a wallboard screw gun and self-tapping metal wallboard screws to attach the wallboard to the steel channel. Adding the insulation and channel to a 2 × 4 wall increases the sound rating from 32 STC to 48 STC. Photo courtesy of Owens/Corning Fiberglas.

Detail shot shows how resilient channel furrs or holds wallboard away from contact with the framing 2 × 4s. The channel is resilient, so it flexes slightly to absorb sound waves, rather than bouncing them back to rooms. Photo courtesy of Owens/Corning Fiberglas.

other functions, or can perform them better, by good planning.

Fireproofing is a good example. The Gypsum Association has performed exhaustive tests so you can engineer a wall or ceiling to be about as fireproof as you could wish. For example, if you use the standard ½″-thick wallboard, you achieve a fire rating of 45 minutes. The fire rating is the time it would take to kindle the wood framing in the wall or ceiling if you applied the heat recorded in a burning building — usually estimated at 1700° F. — to the finished or wallboard side of the surface. If you want better fire resistance, you can apply ⅝″-thick wallboard (called Firecode by USG) and get a fire rating of 60 minutes. If you want a two-hour fire rating, no problem: just apply *two* layers of ⅝″-thick wallboard to any wall or ceiling where you want to increase fire resistance. In common walls between houses and attached garages, for example, building codes require the use of ⅝″-thick wallboard for a one hour fire rating.

Soundproofing is another area where you can engineer performance into a wall or ceiling. You can provide better soundproofing by making the wallboard thicker, or by using multiple layers of wallboard to increase the mass and thus increase the sound performance of the wall or ceiling. For example, an ordinary application where you apply ½″-thick wallboard over the joists will give you a sound transmission class (STC) rating of only 32, a level at which loud speech can be heard through the ceiling or wall. If you install fiberglass batt insulation between the joists, screw resilient steel channel to the joists, then screw ⅝″-thick wallboard to the resilient channels, you will increase the sound rating to a 48 STC, so loud speech will not be heard through the wall or ceiling. By the same token, you can stagger two rows of 2 × 4 studs on both sides of a 2 × 6 plate, then weave fiberglass batt insulation between the studs, and achieve the same 48 STC sound rating. There are also fiberboard panels that can reduce sound transmission through a wall or ceiling. Just nail the soundproofing panels over the studs or joists, then drive longer (2″) wallboard screws through the wallboard and soundproofing panels and into the framing. This combination will yield an STC of 46.

Consider using one of the soundproofing methods mentioned in the section on ceilings to reduce noise transmission between the basement and the first floor. Also consider using sound control between any bedrooms and basement recreation space. Another common sound problem is the plumbing noises which pass through walls between the bathroom and guest or recreation area. Install batt insulation between the studs and pack batt insulation around plumbing pipes to reduce bathroom noises.

Manufacturers of wallboard materials also offer acoustic caulks that can be used to seal cracks against noise passage. Use these caulks under the bottom or sole plates to seal cracks between the sole plates and the floor. Caulk where walls meet, and caulk where openings are cut into the walls for heat ducts or electrical outlets. Remember, any open crack is a potential source of noise. Consider installing exterior door sweeps at the bottom of interior doors, to block noise transfer.

FINISHING WALLBOARD

The goal in finishing wallboard is to conceal all joints, screws, inside corners, and outside corners so they present an unbroken, flat, and attractive surface. To accomplish this one must realize that all wallboard finishing compounds contain a large proportion of water. This water will reduce the volume of the compound as it evaporates from the compound. This means that taping compound is a fairly high-shrink material: multiple coats or applications of taping compound must be applied, allowing time for complete drying between coats, to defeat the shrinkage factor and to achieve a flat, blemish-free wall or ceiling. This shrinkage factor is the reason one must apply three or more coats of compound on each joint or crack. Trying to skip

TOOL LIST
☐ 6″-wide taping knife
☐ 4″-wide taping knife
☐ 10″- and 12″-wide finishing knives
☐ Mud pan
☐ Mud mixer (restaurant potato masher)
☐ Mixing bit for ½″ drill (optional)
☐ Wallboard wet sander
☐ Sanding block, sandpaper (optional)
☐ 5-gallon plastic pail (for washing tools)
☐ Scrub brush

one or more coats of compound will produce an uneven finish, with visible screwheads and "starved" or unfilled joints and outside corner beads. No amount of skill in application will defeat the simple fact that you must apply repeated coats to eliminate the shrinkage of the taping compound.

To begin the taping operation, inspect the wallboard job completely. Have you installed the number of screws recommended by the wallboard adhesive manufacturer? In areas where a vapor barrier prevented use of wallboard adhesives, did you space the screws 12 inches apart? Push against the wallboard: are all panels in complete contact with the framing, with no loose panels? Have you nailed steel corner beads on all outside corners?

If the job seems complete, it is time to start application of the tape and taping compound. I recommend buying ready-mix taping compound for the beginning taper. Dry powder, available in 25-pound bags, is cheaper, and is often the choice of the pro. But there is the problem of mixing the powder so it is smooth and just the proper consistency to be workable and lump-free. Compound that is too thin will result in poor bond between the compound and the tape and tiny cracks along the tape edges, caused by excessive compound shrink-

age. Too-thick compound will set too fast, leaving dry spots and bubbles in the tape. It will be too hard to spread and smooth, making taping a tiresome operation. Ready-mix taping compound is available in one, two, or five-gallon plastic pails. It is mixed to the proper consistency at the factory, and it is mixed with potable (drinkable) water that is free from rust or other materials that might affect the taping compound or leave stains in the compound that will be difficult to cover with paint.

Taping compound is nearly perfect in consistency as it comes from the factory. There may be water separation from the compound so a little liquid is present on top of the pail. Use a stir stick or a restaurant-size potato masher (available from wallboard supply stores) to mix the liquid back into the compound. If the compound still seems thick and difficult to apply, you can thin it slightly, following the directions on the pail. Mix bits that fit into half-inch drills are also available at tool stores. These power-mixers make mixing wallboard compound, texture paints, and asphalt patcher and sealer products much easier. The mix bits are a good investment if you do any amount of home repair yourself.

For applying tape to the wallboard, use a 6″-wide knife for taping joints and spotting screwheads, and use a 4″-wide knife for applying tape to inside corners. Corner taping tools that have two blades mounted to form a 90° angle are available, but they are difficult to use and I suggest that you stick to the 4″ knife.

To carry the taping compound to the walls, use a mud pan designed for that purpose. The mud pan is an enlarged baker's bread pan. It holds a quart or more of taping compound, fits in the palm of the hand for easy carrying, and can be set down on sawhorse or workbench without spilling compound when you are about other tasks. Also available for this purpose is a flat tool with a center handle underneath, called a plasterer's hawk. The hawk is a tool that takes getting used to, and if you set it down while it is loaded with compound, it will either fall over or let the compound slide off the hawk.

For finishing joints and outside corner bead you can choose between flat taping knives, available in 10″ and 12″ widths, and plastering trowels that have handles atop bent metal shanks. If you have not worked with the top-handle type of trowel, we suggest you choose the flat taping knives as more "user friendly" taping tools.

Use the 6″ knife to lift compound out of the plastic pail and into the mud pan. Don't overload the mud pan; it's easier to work light and return to the pail for more compound.

Keep the temperature turned down while you are applying taping compound. Premature drying will interfere with the bond between the compound and the joint tape. You'll find about 60° a more comfortable temperature for working than the higher levels normally thought of as "room temperature."

A common failure for beginners is to take a choppy approach to finishing joints, making repeated attacks with the knife or trowel. These repeated attacks leave a choppy finish that is filled with trowel marks and ridges, and thus increase the task of sanding the compound smooth. Instead, load the taping knife with compound, and spread it the full length of the joint, or as far as the knifeload of compound will allow. Don't try to apply compound to many joints at once, before applying the tape. Apply compound to one joint, smooth it, embed the wallboard tape, then wipe the excess taping compound from under the tape. Then, again using the 6″ knife, butter the next joint with compound, smooth it, embed the tape and wipe the joint smooth. Continue until you have taped all the joints.

Note that in most wallboard finishing jobs you should tape the joints first, then tape the corners or inside angles. This will let the joints dry so you

do not scrape the joint away while you are trying to tape over the joints to finish the inside corners. But this is a judgment call. If you are taping where the ceilings are of uniform height, at a usual 8′ high or slightly less as the basement will be, tape the joints, then go back and tape the corners. If you are taping on high ceilings where scaffold is required, it may make more sense to tape everything as you go to avoid many scaffold moves. If you are working on high ladders and planks in a basement stairwell, for example, you will probably want to tape the joints, then tape the corners, spot nails, etc., so you won't have to keep moving/climbing the scaffold.

After taping all the joints, go back and tape the inside corners or angles. The joint tape has a slight ridge down the center, and you fold the tape at this point to tape the corners. Apply compound to both sides of the corner with the 4″ knife, fold the tape and position it squarely in the corner, then wipe the excess taping compound from both sides of the corner.

The taper's term for finishing screw or nail heads is "spotting." Spot all screw heads by putting a walnut-size dab of taping compound over the fastener, then wipe the material away with a shearing motion. The important thing to remember when spotting nails is that you want to fill only the recessed head area of the fastener: you do not want to leave a mound of material on the wall or ceiling. These mounds of taping compound, often seen on amateur jobs, will stick out like measles when lights are turned on the finished wall. The goal, as elsewhere noted, is to make everything — screwheads, joints, corner beads, everything — flat.

Use the wide taping knife, the 10″ or 12″, to apply compound over the outside corner bead. You will note that the center ridge on the corner bead is still visible after you apply the fill coat of compound. This center ridge or screed serves a double purpose. First, the finish tool rides along the screed and is a guide for the finisher. Second, the metal

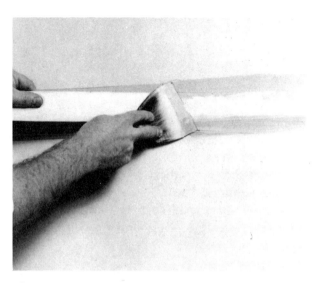

Apply wallboard compound over the joints, then position reinforcing tape on the compound. Use taping knife to embed the tape in the compound and remove any excess compound from the joint. Let compound dry before re-coating. Photo courtesy of United States Gypsum.

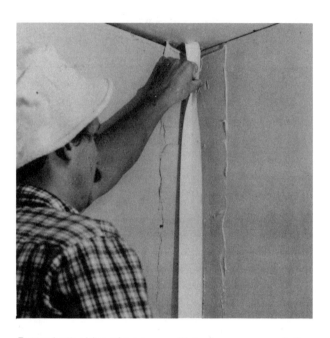

Butter both sides of a corner with taping compound, then fold the tape down the middle and press it into the compound. Use taping knife to remove excess compound and smooth and square tape in the corner. Photo courtesy of Gold Bond Building Products.

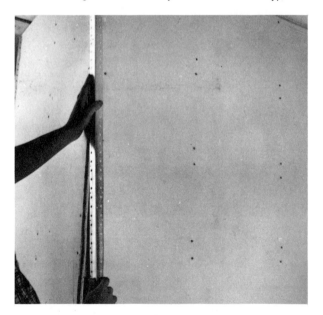

Trim wallboard ends at the corners so they are perfectly square, provide a proper seat for corner bead. Note the double-nailing system on the wallboard nail pattern. The wallboard is first nailed off with one nail in each location, over entire pattern. Workman then returns and drives a second nail close to first nail to be sure panels are tight against framing. Photo courtesy of Gold Bond Building Products.

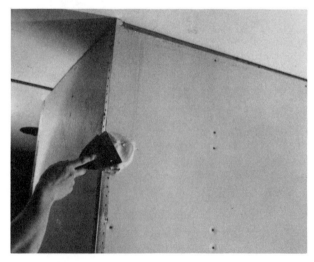

After nailing corner bead in place, apply three coats of wallboard compound to completely fill the corner. Let compound dry completely between each coat. Use wider taping knife or trowel for second and third coats. Photo courtesy of Gold Bond Building Products.

edge is still exposed after finishing, so there is no compound covering the point of the screed. This ensures that the corner will suffer only nicked paint if the corner is bumped after it is finished; and it leaves the bare metal corner to absorb the blow, rather than a covering of soft compound which would surely break away if struck with furniture or toys. So, the point of the corner is designed to be left bare.

Covering the corner bead completes the first phase of the taping operation. Tape is in place to reinforce joints and inside corners; metal corner bead protects and covers outside corners. Let everything dry for at least 24 hours before proceeding. All first coat materials must be perfectly dry in order for full shrinkage to have occurred: putting wet compound over wet compound will result in delayed shrinkage and in effect will constitute only one coat of compound, not two. Be patient and let it dry.

When everything has dried, use the wider 10″ knife to apply a second or leveling coat of compound. Dip the knife into the pan, so taping compound is spread evenly along the front edge of the knife blade. Now apply a thin coat of compound over the joint, feathering the edges to remove any ridges. Again, the key is to pull the knife the full length of the joint in one pass; or, if the joint is full-length of the wall, finish one-half of the joint, starting at one end of the wall, then turn and finish the other half of the joint, starting at the opposite corner. The point is to make the finish strokes as long and uninterrupted as possible, because there will be a ridge in the compound when you stop the finish action.

As you finish the tapered joint edges or recess joints, you can simply cover the joint with compound, then stand the knife on end and scrape away the excess, leaving the recess area full and flat. For end or butt joints, check each joint with a straightedge before troweling it. If the joint is flat, as it should be, you can finish it with the same skimming motion you use on recess joints. But if there is a slight hump in the butt joint, flare or spread the finish compound wide to make the hump a gradual one, not an abrupt change in the flatness or plane of the wall or ceiling.

You do not need to apply two coats to each side of the inside corners. Apply one smoothing coat to each side of the corner to conceal the compound shrinkage at the edges of the tape. Don't try to apply compound to both sides of the corner at once, because you will disturb the fresh compound on the side you just finished. Instead, apply a thin coat of compound to one side of the corner, let it dry, then apply compound to the opposite side of the corner. All inside corners are finished with the 4″ wide knife. A good procedure is to apply compound to one side of the inside corners when you apply the first covering coat over the joints; apply compound to the opposite side of all corners when you apply the second covering coat of compound to the joints.

Be aware that you do not need to sand the compound between coats, if you keep the job clean and free of ridges as you proceed. You will quickly learn it is much easier to wipe away ridges or spills while they are wet, using the finish knives, than to leave blobs of compound to dry in place, then try to remove them with sandpaper. Keep a wallboard wet sander, a sponge with an abrasive cover of nylon, at hand during the finishing process. As the compound starts to set, but before it is completely dry, wipe ridges and knife marks away with the wet sander.

As you finish applying compound to each room, after each coat turn back and use the taping knife to pick up any blobs of compound that were dropped on the floor. Again, the compound is much easier to move while it is still wet; don't let it dry hard and then try to scrape or sand it away.

When all corners are finished, and all screws, joints, and outside corner bead have been covered

Use sanding block with a 4'-long handle and U-joint at head to sand job, including ceilings, from floor. Note dust mask and eye goggles on workman. Always wear eye protection when sanding, cutting or painting. Photo courtesy of Gold Bond Building Products.

Workman shown is applying thin-coat plaster. You can achieve the same effect if you apply a skim coat over the entire wallboard job. Photo courtesy of United States Gypsum.

with three coats of compound, remove the reflector from a trouble light, or the shade from a lamp, and hold the bare lit bulb close to the wall or ceiling. Strong sidelight will accent any problems that remain: hollow areas over recessed screwheads, edge joints that are not full, butt joints that cast shadows should all be recoated. When you are satisfied, wet sand the entire job.

I strongly urge that you use the wet sander, not sandpaper, to smooth the wallboard job. The wet sander is effective if you keep it handy as you proceed and smooth the compound when it is too firm to smear but not yet completely dry. Using sandpaper is a last resort, and most people who have tried doing their own wallboard work list the job of sanding, and the mess and dust it creates, as the most objectionable part of the entire project.

Wallboard manufacturers recommend that you apply a skim or shear coat (not sheer, thin, but shear for the motion of slicing the compound almost completely away, leaving only a very thin film on the surface) over the entire wallboard area. This recommendation makes sense because without it you have a problem in painting the wallboard. The problem is that the screwheads, corners, and joints are coated with taping compound, while the field (the rest of the wallboard) is covered only with the face or finish paper. When you apply paint to such a surface, you obviously will have a difference in the paint, because it will lie differently on the compound areas than on the areas where you are painting bare paper. The problem is, this skim or covering coat is difficult for most people to do, and it's a lot of work. However, it is recommended, and it is a good procedure to use, especially in areas where you would like to use gloss paint for high washability. To test your own skills, try skim coating the bathroom, where you might like to use gloss enamel for moisture resistance and easy cleaning.

When you have finished the wallboard job, the best paint for a first coat is a high-solids latex.

Another good option as a base coat is a product from United States Gypsum called "First Coat." A latex-base product, it is available either already mixed, or in powder form to be mixed with water. It can be a cheap alternative to more costly primers or sealers, and it does the best job of evening out the surface suction, or absorption rate, of the paint.

One word of warning. Oil or alkyd base primers and sealers are not suitable as a first coat over wallboard, and have never been recommended by the manufacturers. That is because the slow-drying oil-base paints soak into the face paper of the wallboard and lift the nap on the paper. When the primer or sealer dries, these fuzzy paper particles are locked in an upright position, and leave a rough surface on the wallboard. Latex paints, on the other hand, are quick-drying and "lay the nap" or make the paper fibers lie down so the wallboard is smooth. The only place where alkyd or oil base primers can be used as a first coat over wallboard is on ceilings that will receive a rough spray texture. Even on ceilings that will be textured, there is no need for using alkyds: USG recommends their First Coat latex as the primary coat over new wallboard, regardless of the finish you plan for the walls or ceilings.

CLEANUP

You can reseal the plastic pails of compound for later use. When you are through for the day, use a scrub brush to wipe down the sides of the plastic compound pail. Cover the surface of the compound so air cannot reach and dry it. When you are ready to resume work, pour the excess water from the top of the compound and stir in the top moisture.

Set taping tools in a plastic scrub pail when you are not using them, so taping compound will not dry on the tools. Wash the tools with a scrub brush before putting them away. Don't pour compound down the sewer drain: place compound in the trash for disposal.

OWNER'S INSPECTION CHECKLIST — DRYWALL (WALLBOARD)

NOTES

✓ Before application begins, check that all wiring, plumbing, framing are in place. Make final check of insulation and vapor barrier.

✓ Insist on premier installation techniques. All wallboard applied perpendicular to framing; 1″ wallboard screws as fasteners; wallboard adhesive used in all areas where there is no vapor barrier.

_____ Be sure no vapor barrier is added in bath areas where water resistant wallboard is used. Vapor barrier under water resistant board is prohibited by manufacturers.

_____ Water resistant board will sag if used on ceilings. Use regular wallboard for bath ceilings.

✓ All-metal, nail-on corner beads to be used on all outside corners. Glue-on corner bead can be easily damaged by impact blows.

✓ All outside corner bead, joints, nail or screw heads to receive not less than three (3) coats of taping/finishing compound. Texture paint will not flatten or "hide" joints with excess shrinkage or two coat finish. — *ASKED FOR THIRD COAT 7/2*

_____ Spray texture ceilings will look better if they receive a first coat of primer. Prime coat ceilings before spraying.

_____ Check textured surfaces for uniform appearance, complete coverage. Check texture from several angles to find skips or "holidays" in texture.

✓ At night, with lights out, apply strong sidelight to walls, using trouble light with bare bulb held near wall. Look down the wall and check for hollow nail or screw heads, hollow or "starved" joints, loose or bubbled tape, rough edges. This inspection is most easily done after walls are primed.

✓ Mark any blemishes or rough spots with a pencil, so you can find them in daylight. Do not use a ballpoint pen or a marker for this step: the ink or dye bleeds through most paints, making it difficult to hide.

✓ Check inside corners to be sure they are square, not loaded with taping compound. Corners that are not square make trim application difficult.

✓ Save large scraps of wallboard for future repairs. — *IN LARGE CLOSET*

_____ Some drywall contractors do not cover new wallboard, but instead overspray at the corners, then scrape away the texture on the walls. Check to be sure the scraping process has left the corners smooth, without piles of texture at corners to interfere with wall decoration.

9
Doors and Trim

TOOL LIST

- ☐ Pencil, No. 2 lead (sharp)
- ☐ Miter box & saw
- ☐ Coping saw
- ☐ Prybar(s)
- ☐ Drill, assorted bits
- ☐ Measuring tape
- ☐ Hammer, 14 oz. finish
- ☐ Nail set
- ☐ Wood chisel(s), sharp
- ☐ Carpenter's level
- ☐ Handsaw
- ☐ Carpenter's glue (white)
- ☐ Razor knife
- ☐ Circular saw
- ☐ Straightedge
- ☐ Screwdriver(s)
- ☐ Clamps
- ☐ Nail bag, tool belt
- ☐ Beeswax (to lubricate nails)

Before ordering the finish products for your basement, consider the architectural style of the house. For continuity, you may want to use panel or lou-vered doors, and wider trim, to match the existing style. Sliding or bi-fold doors (doors that fold ac-cordion-style) take up little room because they do not swing on a hinge as ordinary doors do. The cheapest doors are the familiar hollow-core doors, but if you have panel doors upstairs, you may want to match them. Plus, younger adults who grew up with hollow-core slab doors are finding that panel doors offer a more gracious and attractive appear-ance. Some are using the hollow-core doors and adding molding to the doors for style; an inexpen-sive way of getting the more intricate, and some think more interesting look.

CLOSET DOORS

For any closet (except cedar-lined) I recommend using louvered doors. The louvers permit air cir-culation, making them doubly important in any basement that has high humidity. Louvered doors are also suggested for laundry rooms, for the same reason: air circulation helps prevent a buildup of humidity and all the problems that humidity causes.

Consider using floor-to-ceiling, louvered bi-fold or sliding doors on closets. These are available in painted steel or in fiberglass. The doors are light-weight, inexpensive when you consider they don't require painting or staining, and are easily installed. Usually, these doors slide on an overhead track that is screwed to the ceiling joists; a pivot pin in the bottom of the doors fits into a socket that is attached to the floor with two screws. The metal or fiberglass doors will not warp or swell in the humidity as wood doors may.

If you have no moisture problems you may opt for the look of wood doors for closets. Again, go for the louvered look to aid air circulation. If you plan the door openings carefully, you should have little trouble installing the wood doors: they are cut to fit, and are pre-bored for top and base hardware. If you are going to have an aromatic-cedar closet, use a pre-hung door and apply the thin cedar boards to the closet side of the door. You can either set the cedar panels back from the edge of the door, so it will still swing and close against the door stop, or you can do it the pro way and reset the door hinges to allow for the extra added thickness of the cedar planks you have added to the inside of the door.

PREHUNG DOORS

Doors for passage into the bedrooms and bath come prehung, which means they are set in the door frame, the hinges are attached, and one side of the trim is already attached to the jamb. Your job is to set the unit into the opening, plumb and level the jamb with a carpenter's level, then use finish nails to secure the unit in the rough opening. Use 6d or 8d finish nails to secure the unit. Use cedar shims, available in packages at your lumber yard, to shim the door jamb in the opening. Drive the nails through the side jambs at the hinge and lock locations. This will provide maximum support for the door at the points of greatest stress. Nail also through the trim that is already attached to the unit, then position and nail the trim on the opposite side of the jamb. Note the trim already

attached to the door is set back about ¼″ from the edge of the jamb: set the loose trim back the same distance from the door side or inside of the jamb. An easy way to do this is to use a combination square as a guide. Slide the rule in the square handle so the rule extends just ¼″ past the 90° side of the handle. Tighten the clamp in the handle so the rule won't slip. Set this ¼″ edge on the door jamb and align the trim against the end of the rule. This provides a uniform spacer or gauge so you can set the trim back an equal distance on all sides of the jamb. The last step is to install the lockset in the pre-drilled hole. This requires only four screws, which are provided with the lockset. If you are installing the door on a bathroom, buy a lockset with an unlock feature so you can open the door in an emergency or if a child locks himself in the bathroom. This type of lock usually has a hole in the knob on the outside, and a small pin or pick that can be inserted in the knob hole to unlock the door. Place the lock pick on the trim ledge at the top of the door, to keep it handy should an emergency arise.

CUTTING OFF A DOOR

Because basement ceiling height is limited, and there are further limitations because of steel or wood beams that limit headroom, you may have to cut off the bottoms of the doors to fit into low openings. If the door is solid wood, cutting it off is no problem; in the case of prefinished doors you may have to adjust headers over the tops of the door openings to fit 80″ doors beneath.

Cutting off a prehung, hollow-core door is a fairly easy job, once you know the procedure. Use a screwdriver to drive the hinge pins from the hinges, then remove the door and lay it flat atop a pair of sawhorses. Note and mark the bottom of the door: with the door off the hinges, it is easy to become confused and cut off the wrong (top) end. Remember before you start cutting that the door is shipped with an average ¾″ gap at the bottom, so it will swing over most carpets without being cut. Allow for that ¾″ existing gap when you measure how much to cut off.

Mark your cutoff point and clamp a straight edge such as a wallboard T-square or a straight piece of lumber to the door as a cutting guide for your saw. Now use a sharp razor knife to cut through the thin veneer on both sides of the door. Make repeated cuts with the knife until you are sure you have cut completely through the veneer. Put a plywood or paneling blade in your circular saw. Cutting through the face veneer and using a paneling blade will help prevent the veneer from splitting as you saw it. Carefully make your saw cut, being careful not to snag the saw's cord on the door and cause a miscut in the door.

When you remove the cutoff portion of the door, you may see that you have cut away the entire frame at the door's bottom, leaving the hollow core (hole) of the door exposed. If the opening is exposed, you will see corrugated cardboard that is woven in a crooked pattern in the hollow area. There is glue on both sides of this cardboard, to glue the spacer to both side veneers. You must use the razor knife to cut away this cardboard, for a distance about 2″ up into the hollow core.

When you have prepared the door opening, use a sharp chisel to peel the veneer off both sides of the cutoff portion of the door. This veneer will usually peel off with little urging, because the glue is brittle and lets the veneer pop away easily. Use the sharp edge of the chisel to cut away all glue residue from this frame piece.

When you have removed the veneer from the frame, test fit the frame piece into the hole in the bottom of the door. The frame should slip snugly but easily into the hole, without being forced. When you are sure you have a fit between the frame and the door hollow, apply carpenter's glue to the frame piece sides. Now slip the frame into the open core of the door, and secure it in place with C-clamps until the glue dries.

If you have removed 2 inches or more of the door, enough to have penetrated into the hollow core, you will also have to cut the door frame or jamb. Cut carefully, leaving the side jambs ¾″ longer than the door. If the door must be even shorter, cutting off too much of a prehung unit will lower the door knob and drop the bottom hinge location to an unacceptable degree. Have a millwork company build custom doors for the height needed, or call in a pro carpenter who can build, hang, and lock the door for you.

TRIM

Trim or trim moldings are designed to finish off cracks that occur between ceilings and walls; between walls and floors, other walls, or cabinets; and between door or window frames or jambs and the adjoining wall. Trim lumber is available in a wide variety of shapes to fit any need. Ask your lumber dealer to help you select the trim you need for any job. Many dealers display a sample board, showing base moldings, casings, inside and outside corner moldings, quarter-round, cap molding for the top of wainscoting, and sprung or cove molding for the corner between wall and ceilings.

It's a good idea to pre-drill molding to avoid splitting the molding during nailing. If you do much finish work, you will enjoy using a 14 oz. finish hammer, rather than the heavier 16 oz. hammer, for fine finish work. Use a nail set to drive the nail below the surface of the wood, then putty the nail hole(s).

Don't overnail molding(s). Too many nails will pull the molding into the irregular curves in a wall or ceiling, and the eye tends to follow the molding. Nailing about every 16″ is right. When nailing base molding, drive the nails into the wall, not into the floor. If you have a hardwood floor, you must leave the flooring strips free to expand and contract: nailing into the flooring prevents free floor movement during expansion.

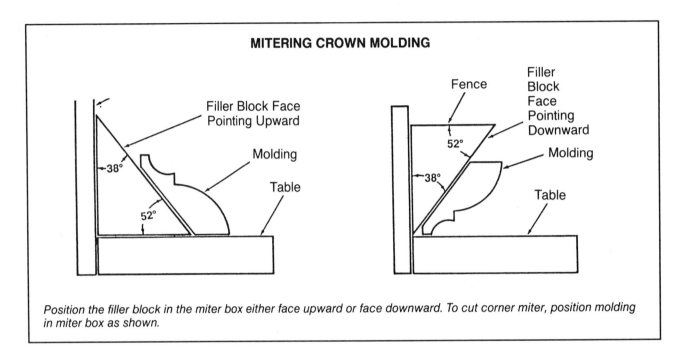

MITERING CROWN MOLDING

Position the filler block in the miter box either face upward or face downward. To cut corner miter, position molding in miter box as shown.

Chair railing is often used on a wall to cover the crack between wood wainscoting on the bottom of the wall and plaster or wallboard above. Chair railing can also be used to make a decorative accent. Nail chair railing at 32″ above the floor, and hang wallcovering on the top, with paint on the lower one-third of the wall. Or, a stained chair railing can be a high impact item, just nailed at 32″ height on a wall that is painted all one color.

You can create a heavy crown molding between a wall and ceiling by using a combination of two, three, or more pieces of trim. For example, if you nail a 2 × 2 nailing block into a corner, then install one piece of sprung cove molding between the ceiling and 2 × 2, and another piece between the wall and the 2 × 2, you can make a very attractive deep cove molding.

Cutting Miters

One necessary requirement for installing molding is to have a high-quality miter saw, or a hollow-ground blade in a radial arm or table saw. You simply cannot cut accurately enough to do trim work without a good miter saw. The cheapie wood or plastic miter boxes will not do: even a slight miscut, off a degree or two, will result in a very amateurish-looking job. If you must, rent a miter box and saw, but don't attempt to cut trim without one.

Cutting miters, assuming you have an accurate saw, is not very difficult. For picture frame moldings, or most casing for door and window trim, you simply must swing the miter saw to 45°, right or left, as the cut requires. Quality miter saws have positive stops that let you lock the saw firmly at 22½° and 45°, either right or left.

For fitting baseboard, set the base molding upright in the miter box. For outside corners, just cut the ends of the two pieces at a 45° angle, right and left. For cutting joints at mid-wall, cut the ends of baseboard or base shoe at parallel 45° angles, so they form an overlapping or "scarf" joint.

Cutting miters in crown moldings can be confusing. The easiest way to be sure the miter fits is to cut a filler block and place it against the back of the miter box (fence). Most crown moldings have 52° and 38° contact surfaces on the rear of the molding. You must maintain these angles when the crown molding joins the face of the filler block. The first step is to rip a 2 × 4 block or similar scrap into a right triangle in which one angle is 38°, the second angle is the reciprocal of 38°, or 52°. (In a right triangle, one angle is 90°; the other two, added together, must total 90°. Thus, 38° plus 52° = 90°.) When you position the filler block in the miter box with the block face, or hypothenuse of the triangle, pointing down, you can set the crown molding in the box with the top or ceiling side of the molding up, and make your miter cut.

If you are working with molding, the key point is that you must remember the attitude or position of the molding *when it is in place on the wall or ceiling.* Many mistakes with molding or trim installation are due to the fact that the worker just laid the molding flat in the miter box, and cut the miter angle. This works only on picture-type molding and door or window trim. Base molding must be set upright in the miter box; crown molding is cut with a filler block to hold it at the right angle.

TRIM TIPS

A common problem is finding that a corner is not flat and door or window trim won't match at corner miters. Options include sticking small wood shims between the trim and the wallboard to hold one or both corners out from the wall so the miters match. Another trick is to use a prybar to hold both miter ends so they are aligned. Apply white glue to the joint. Now drive a nail downward, through the top trim piece, into the leg below, being sure the two corners align when the nail penetrates into the second member or leg of the trim. Remove the prybar and let the trim pieces move back where they will. Any small crack between the wall and trim can be ignored, or can be filled with a dab of caulk or wallboard compound.

Another trick is to use a *very* sharp chisel to cut away the edge of the trim at the miter cut. Using the chisel like a small plane, make repeated cuts that taper the edge of the trim toward the joint, so there is no offset between the two members at the joint. If the edges appear to line up, then the joint will seem flat.

One should never set a side trim for a door on the floor, then mark and cut the miter at the top. Instead, cut a miter angle of 45° on a piece of side trim that is longer than the finished leg or side trim will be. When you have a sharp miter cut, turn the trim piece upside down, with the sharp point of the miter resting lightly on the floor (don't damage the sharp point of the miter). Now, make a mark where the top of the side trim meets the top edge of the top trim. Make your straight 90° cut on the end that will sit on the floor. This way, any miscut will result in a slight crack at the floor/side trim joint, not at the miter joint.

Does your trim work often result in open miter joints, with a slight but even crack at the miter? That indicates that your saw may not be cutting true on the perpendicular cuts. To avoid open joints, and ensure joints that will be watertight, backcut the edge on the back corner of the miter cut. Using a small block plane or a sharp chisel, cut away the edge of the miter, on the back side. This will ensure that the face edges can come together in an almost invisible joint.

OWNER'S INSPECTION CHECKLIST — TRIM AND DOORS

Trim

✓ All trim is in place, including base, shoe, moldings, stops.

✓ Chair rails, crown moldings in place as specified.

✓ All joints are clean-cut and tight-fitting. Miter joints are tight and well-fit, both re the wall surfaces and the adjoining trim.

_____ Fireplace mantel is installed and finished.

✓ Trim is grade specified and free of blemishes or defects.

✓ Nails are set below trim surface.

✓ All paneling and shelving is in place and finished per specifications.

✓ Stair rails, balusters, stringers are in place and well anchored. Treads are solid and squeak-free.

Doors

✓ All doors correct size, style, and type.

✓ Doors swing freely and quietly. Open doors will remain in any position without moving.

✓ Door knobs, latches, and hinges are properly set and aligned. Latches align with latch plates.

✓ Any exterior door(s) lock properly, open easily.

_____ All exterior door locks are keyed alike, to avoid dealing with multiple keys.

✓ All doors open in correct direction, i.e., right or left hand. NOTE: Stand inside room so door will open towards you. If knob is on right hand side, it's a right hand door; if knob is on left hand side, it's a left hand door. Remember: Door must open *toward* you in this test.

✓ Doors are plumb against their jambs. Check crack around door for even fit and good alignment.

✓ Nails are set below surface of trim; no hammer dents or split wood; miter joints fit tightly.

✓ Any thresholds are installed and properly adjusted.

✓ Any exterior doors are weather stripped.

✓ Door bottom is at right height for good clearance over carpet, tile, etc.

_____ Door stops are properly set so door fits snugly against stop but latches without force.

✓ Exterior doors are fitted with deadbolt locks for security.

NOTES

RE-KEY KITCHEN DOOR TO MATCH

CHECK EXT. DOOR FOR SWELLING AFTER RAIN

10
Painting

TOOL LIST

- ☐ Ladder(s)
- ☐ Brushes, 1″, 2″, 4″
- ☐ Roller frame, 9″
- ☐ 2′ and 4′ roller extension handles
- ☐ Assorted roller covers
- ☐ Stir sticks
- ☐ Sandpaper
- ☐ Wood putty
- ☐ Plastic drop cloths
- ☐ Tack or wipe cloths
- ☐ Sponges
- ☐ Wash pail, plastic
- ☐ Wire brush (for concrete)
- ☐ Patching trowels
- ☐ Scrapers, taping knives
- ☐ Masking tape
- ☐ Eye goggles
- ☐ Dust masks
- ☐ Rubber gloves
- ☐ Cup sprayer
- ☐ Caulking gun, caulks

Because the basement often has limited air circulation, it's a good practice to use factory-finished materials whenever possible. Cabinets, paneling, trim and molding, suspended ceilings, and ceiling tile are all examples of materials that are finished so you can "nail the paint on" as you apply the materials. Unfinished trim and millwork can be stored in a sheltered area such as a garage and can be stained and sealed before being moved into the basement. It is also true that most people will find latex finishes less objectionable than alkyd or oil base finishes. If you have family members who have allergies, pay particular attention to the finish paints you choose. Provide as much ventilation and air circulation as possible during painting. It is best to augment ventilation with fans to ensure proper drying and ventilation.

TEXTURE PAINTS

Texture paints provide decorating interest, pattern and variety to walls and ceilings. In addition, rough-textured finishes break up lighting and create shadows that can help conceal less-than-perfect surfaces. Textures also provide better acoustics than smooth walls because they help eliminate the sound bounce that is common in

Sheetrock™ First Coat is a latex-based primer product that is specially formulated to eliminate such wallboard problems as joint banding and shadowing. The product is available ready-mixed, or as a powder that must be mixed with water. The application shown is by airless sprayer: First Coat can be applied by brush, roller, or spray. Never use oil-based paints or primers as a first coat on wallboard. Photo courtesy of United States Gypsum Co.

Decorative wall textures are available in either a paste or sand-float (see photo, page 113) finish. To ease decorating chores, prime wall with USG's First Coat or high-solids latex paint to stop drying by wall absorption. Using a humidifier in the room also slows drying by evaporation, increases "open time" for texture paint. Photos courtesy of United States Gypsum Co.

This photo shows contrast between two types of spray textures. On the ceiling, the coarse aggregate provides hiding power, decorative effect, and improved sound control. On the wall, spatter-texture provides a high-hide finish for wallboard construction without the high aggregate ceiling effect that might be too much texture if applied to a wall. Photo courtesy of Gold Bond Building Products.

areas with smooth, hard-finish paint surfaces.

Some texture finishes have better acoustic value than others. True acoustic textures never harden, but offer a perpetually soft finish that absorbs rather than reflects sound waves. The drawback to acoustic textures is that the soft finish (which resembles play dough) cannot be cleaned or repainted with any paint other than another application of the texture material. Obviously, acoustic textures must be applied by pros, because they must be applied with spray equipment. Keep in mind that ordinary interior paints will leave a hard surface film on textures, so they either reduce or destroy completely the ability of the texture to absorb sound waves. You should never apply ordinary paint over acoustic texture or acoustic tile ceilings because the paint will end their effectiveness as sound control barriers.

Common wallboard texture paints are adequate for most basement ceilings. The rough ceilings common in most homes today, with a finish made up of aggregates or sand-like "bumps," must be applied with sprayers. The bumps or aggregate are usually lightweight particles of perlite. The lightweight aggregate will tend to pile up, or be deposited on walls or ceilings unevenly, if you try to use rollers or paint brushes to apply them.

Other types of texture paint can be applied with a roller, brush, sponge or any of a number of other tools. Many do-it-yourselfers who have tried applying texture paint complain of a difficult job and poor results. Because of their consistency, texture paints are not easy to apply, but using pro techniques can make the job possible. For the beginner, it is best to stick with the latex-base finishes. Some of these ready-mix finishes have a paste-like consistency that provides the texture appearance, while others also contain sand or perlite for a sand-texture type finish. Choose whichever finish you desire, but don't try to buy the texture paint in the color you would like it. It is easier, and you will obtain a more even color finish, if you concentrate

your first efforts on getting the type of texture pattern you desire, using white texture paint. Then, when the texture paint is dry, apply a coat of latex paint over the textured surface in whatever color pleases you. This will result in a more uniform color in addition to better washability.

The primary problems with applying texture paint result from the thick paint drying prematurely, so you don't have time to texture or pattern it. This problem is due both to the paste-like consistency of the texture paint, and to the fact that, unlike smooth paint, you first need to distribute the material evenly over the surface, then you must turn back and use another tool to make the texture pattern. This two-stage application means that texture painting is a job for two people, so you should enlist a helper either to apply and distribute the material on the surface, or to follow along and do the finish work. The work will go twice as fast, so you will have reduced the time the paint must remain "open" or workable.

The next tip is that the warmer the air and the surface you are texturing, the faster the material will dry. You must therefore turn down the heat so that you are working in no more than 60° temperature. Likewise, the texture paint dries by the water either being absorbed into the surface or by evaporating the water into the air. In addition to reducing the temperature, you should increase the humidity to slow drying of the texture paint. Place one or more humidifiers in the work space and crank humidity levels up to slow evaporation of water from the texture paint.

Test the wall or ceiling surface to see how well it is sealed. As indicated in the wallboard section, the first coat of paint on new wallboard should be either a high-solids latex or Sheetrock® First Coat. Either of these base coats should give you an adequate seal so that water from the texture paint is not absorbed into the wallboard. For texturing old, previously painted surfaces, first apply an alkyd primer to ensure a complete seal, with no absorption of water from the texture paint into the wallboard surface.

When you have the humidity up and the temperature down, you are ready to apply the texture paint. It is best to experiment first on a piece of scrap wallboard or on cardboard, to be sure you can make the exact pattern you want. Most hand-tooled textures are done by first applying a heavy coat of the texture compound to the surface, and spreading it so it is evenly distributed. This initial application is usually done with a long-nap roller or with a fiber brush. When a small area, about 2' × 2', is coated, the helper should start to use the pattern tool to establish the chosen pattern. A stipple finish is done by moving a paint roller with a long nap over the wet texture paint. The roller makes waves on the surface of the texture. The degree of roughness of the stipple texture depends on (1) how much material you pile onto the surface; (2) the type of roller you use (there are special texture rollers); and (3) how wet the texture paint is. If the paint has started to dry, you will not be able to pull a sharp pattern with it.

A sponged effect can be achieved with a natural or plastic sponge. The dry sponge can be dabbed at the wet texture paint, leaving the sponge impression. Dipping the sponge into texture paint and dabbing it on the wet texture wall will produce a different effect; if you wait until the first coat dries, then come back and dab the wall with a sponge filled with texture paint, you will get another variation in pattern.

Other types of texture pattern can be done using a trowel (to pile on more material for a heavy adobe effect), a brush, a comb, crumpled newspaper or burlap, or scrap carpeting tacked to a wood block. The author once textured a game room using cookie cutters made in the shape of the four playing card suits. When pressed into the wet texture paint, the shapes of hearts, diamonds, spades, and clubs yielded an impression that was uniquely suited (no pun intended) for a card-club retreat.

STAINING TRIM

You can accomplish two goals if you stain wood trim before you bring it into the basement. First, doing the staining in a garage will keep the odors out of the house. You can also save a great deal of time and effort by staining the trim lumber before you nail it on the walls.

Wood stains are water-like in consistency, so they can be difficult to bring to the work surface without drips and runs. To avoid all the drawbacks of staining, place the trim pieces across two or more sawhorses to raise them to working height and to keep them off the floor and away from dust. Pour stain into a roller tray, being sure the stain is thoroughly mixed. (You should stir wood stains often as you work, because the color pigments tend to settle out and collect on the bottom of the container. This settling leaves the stain short on pigment and will often cause the stain color to be uneven.) Now put on a pair of rubber gloves to protect your skin from the stain. Use a closed cell sponge to apply the stain to the wood. Dip the sponge in the roller tray to load it with stain. Then wipe the stain onto the wood and smooth it, all in one motion. Using the sponge speeds the staining process because you do not apply the stain and then wipe it to even it out in separate steps. With the sponge you wipe it on and distribute it evenly in one pass. Using a sponge applicator on the uncut trim also reduces time that would be spent in carefully cutting the stain in so you would keep it off the walls. You can make your own stains by adding universal tints or dark-colored paint to mineral spirits. Because this is not scientific, it would be difficult to mix more stain that would be an exact match. If you mix your own stain, mix enough to do the entire job (or at least an entire room) so you don't have to mix and match more stain in mid-project.

PAINT SPRAYERS

Because moisture builds up in a basement, and ventilation is often inadequate, you may want to use louvered doors in the basement, particularly on closets and storage rooms. Louvers are difficult to paint or stain, and you may want to use spray equipment to make finishing louvers less difficult. A hand-held, cup spray gun is perfect for finishing louvers, heat ducts, or any surface that is not smooth. To keep paint or stain fumes out of the house, remove doors or heat registers to the garage and place them on sawhorses for support. As you spray paint or stain on louvers, the spray material tends to run or sag. Keep a clean, dry paintbrush handy, and wipe away paint runs or sags immediately. Letting the louvered doors or registers lie flat during the drying period helps stop stain or paint from running. It is a good idea to let fresh-painted objects set for a few minutes, then return to them to check for runs. Again, pick up paint runs with a clean dry paintbrush.

PUTTYING NAILHOLES

After staining, apply the trim or molding. After you nail on the trim, apply a coat of sealer or polyurethane. Then fill the nailholes with putty. Wood putty is available in a variety of colors and wood tones, or you can buy clear putty and add a little of your own stain to it. When thoroughly mixed, this putty should perfectly match the stain on your trim.

Nailholes in trim are easier to conceal if you drive the nails into grain marks on the trim. The other trick is to match the putty color to the wood stain. Roll a bit of wood putty into a small ball, and push it into the nailhole with your thumb. As you push down on the putty, give your thumb a slight twist: this makes a neat application of the putty, leaving the nailhole full and clean.

When you are using oil-base wood putty, you must always apply the stain and sealer before putting

the nails. Putting oil putty into unsealed wood lets the oil from the putty leach into the wood around the nailhead, where it will leave a circle of oil stain around the nailhole.

Use fine sandpaper or steel wool to smooth the wood trim between coats. Stain or sealer may lift the wood fibers; dust or lint can settle on fresh paint and mar it. Always remember to turn the thermostat down so forced-air furnace blowers do not blow lint and dust around during the finish painting process. Also, keep a shop vac handy and pick up any dust you create immediately, before the furnace blower fan draws the dirt into the furnace or circulates it through the work area.

PAINTING CONCRETE FLOORS

In the past only oil base paints were used for coating basement floors. The oil base paints were prone to peeling, but they were still the best choice because latex paints lacked durability and could not hold up to foot traffic. Today, the acrylic base of latex paints makes them tough enough that latex paint is now the preferred coating for concrete floors. If you follow the directions given, you should get a long-lasting durable finish. The directions here are for a particular brand of latex concrete floor paint, Drylok paint by United Gilsonite Laboratories (UGL). Use these directions as a guideline, but read the label directions on your own paint if directions differ with these, because the manufacturer of the paint will prefer that you follow his directions in order to enforce his product guarantee.

A starting precaution: No paint will hold up if the floor surface is subject to continual wetting from water that is forced up through the floor or through the cracks between the perimeter of the floor slab and the concrete walls. You must take steps to keep water out of the basement before painting the floor. See the information on basement waterproofing in Chapter 1.

Make a child's room irresistibly appealing with wallcoverings or accents such as the Sea-Scape design shown here, from Decorate It! The vinyl accents are applied with 3M's Post-It note adhesives, so they are easy to apply and endlessly changeable. Photo courtesy of Decorate It!

Wall shelving, hangers hold clothes or toys for added color, decorator appeal. Small child will quickly adapt to new room if it looks like home. Photo courtesy of Clairson International.

When you are sure the floor is dry and will stay that way, remove any dust, dirt, oil, or oil residue from sweeping compound. Also, clean away any loose or peeling floor paint or crumbling masonry. If the floor cannot be cleaned with detergent washing, or if the floor has been troweled to a shine, apply UGL's etching compound or a 5% solution of muriatic acid to the floor to clean and etch (to roughen the floor surface with the corrosive acid) the surface. Use UGL's Clear Concrete Protector or a like primer product to seal any bare spots, or the entire floor if you have any doubts about its condition. You can also sand very glossy paint to dull it for recoating.

When you have sanded, etched, and primed the floor, stir the paint thoroughly. Use only water to thin latex paint and do not exceed one pint of water per gallon of paint when thinning. The first coat of paint on unpainted surfaces should be brushed on, and spread well to ensure a good bond with the surface. Allow to dry overnight, then apply a second coat by brush or roller. These tough acrylic floor paints can be damp mopped after 24 hours, scrubbed in one week, and will stand heavy foot traffic after 24 hours. Remember, though, if you use the paint on a concrete garage floor, such as in a tuck-under basement garage, you should not let a car stand on the uncured paint for at least five days.

NON-TOXIC PAINTS

A New Mexico company imports and sells non-toxic paint and other home products from Germany. Livos Plantchemistry offers a variety of paints and stains that are guaranteed non-toxic. In addition to interior and exterior paint products, Livos also offers such items as furniture and shoe polish, wax crayons made of natural waxes and earth pigments, resin and oil finishes that can be used for interior or exterior wood application as well as being used for stone or metal surfaces. Available for use with many of Livos' paint products is their Leinos Citrus Thinner, a non-toxic solvent that can also serve as a brush and tool cleaner.

If you or a member of your family is sensitive to ordinary paints, call or write the folks at Livos. Their address and toll-free phone number are:

> Livos Plantchemistry
> 1365 Rufina Circle
> Santa Fe, NM 87501
> (800) 621-2591
> FAX: (505) 438-0199

OWNER'S INSPECTION CHECKLIST — PAINTING

NOTES

✓ All wallboard to be primed with USG First Coat or heavy-bodied latex paint. Finish coat to be quality latex of prescribed gloss level — flat, semi or high gloss.

✓ Check walls for coverage, neatness, corners neatly cut in to present a straight appearance.

✓ Insist that the painter will spackle any blemishes overlooked by drywall taper, or nicks and scratches on walls inflicted during trim and finish steps.

✓ Check all painted surfaces to be sure the paint is evenly applied: no lap marks, roller ridges, or brush marks permitted.

✓ Check trim, paneling, and cabinetry for paint spatters and runs.

✓ All trim to be at least two coats, nail holes to be puttied.

✓ Slip the foot from a pair of pantyhose over your hand, and move the covered hand over the finished wood. There should be no snags or rough spots.

✓ Check door edges, and top and bottom ends, to be sure they are sealed so moisture cannot penetrate.

✓ Check attention to detail. Check inside of cabinet doors, cabinet and closet shelves, being sure nothing has been skipped.

✓ Check hardware, ceramic tile, and countertops for paint runs and spatters. Insist they be cleaned.   *CLEAN SPOTS ON BATHROOM TILE*

✓ Leftover paint to remain for future touchup. Unused full gallons to be returned and credited to owner's account (some special color mixes cannot be returned).   *IN LARGE CLOSET*

___ Check wallcoverings for pattern match, closed seams, uniformity of color and pattern.

___ Inspect wallcovering job from oblique (angled) lighting for perspective. This will reveal any adhesive or other stains on the surface of the covering.

___ Buy and save at least one roll of each wallcovering pattern, for future repairs. This ensures the material will not be "out of stock" if you need it in the future.

___ Colors can be deceiving. If you find a color you've chosen does not appear true to the color chart once it's on the wall or ceiling, do not insist on immediate repainting. Live with the job for several days, checking the color in changing light conditions, because color can change dramatically with the time of day and type of lighting.

✓ Keep a diary of your job and record the brand and color of paint, the name and stock number of wallcovering, brand and color of ceramic tile, carpet, etc. Keep the book for reference and update it as you redecorate. When you sell the house, it is a welcome gift to the new owner.   *IN FILE CABINET UNDER "BASEMENT"*

11
No-Mess
Options

As noted in the Paint section (Chapter 10), there are materials that will help you finish any space with a minimum of time, mess, and effort. If you are sensitive to paints and adhesives, or if you simply can't stand a mess, or you'd like a quick fix with a minimum of time and effort expended, consider using some or all of the prefinished options available.

WOOD PANELING

Wood paneling is available in 4 × 8 sheets or panels, in thicknesses of 3/16" or ¼". The panels are available in a variety of finishes and wood tones, but I suggest you stick with lighter tones for the basement, where natural light is limited. Dark paneling in an already dark basement is a mistake.

If you choose these thinner 3/16" or ¼" thick panels, you should first apply a layer of ⅜" thick wallboard or gypsum lath or backer board as a base for stiffening the paneling. Prefinished panels resist impact damage best if they are backed up by a gypsum wallboard base.

Wood paneling offers wide decorative choices between a variety of popular wood tones and patterned finishes. Paneling also provides the maximum in durability for high traffic areas such as

Prefinished paneling and a suspended ceiling provide a quick cover-up over basement ceiling water pipes or other obstructions. Note the paneling was applied first, then the suspended ceiling. This ensures that the ceiling will completely cover the wall panels with no gaps, plus it eliminates having to cut all the wall paneling for length. Note that the plywood panels are applied over a wallboard base for greater strength and impact resistance. Photo courtesy of Armstrong World Industries, Inc.

halls, stairways, or game rooms, plus the panels require almost no maintenance. You should apply a paneling treatment such as the clean-and-wax products designed for paneling, as often as needed – more often in high contact areas such as stairways, less often in dens.

Paneling can be cut and installed with ordinary household tools. A circular saw and paneling blade, a saber saw with a fine blade, and an electric drill are all the power tools you will need. The recommendation to use a fine blade, or a circular saw blade designed for paneling, is intended to help you avoid splintering of the paneling face. These blades have numerous fine teeth so they cut more smoothly than a combination blade does.

You can also cut paneling with a hand saw. Because of the direction of cut, you should always cut paneling with the face side up when using a hand saw, and with the face side down when using a circular saw or saber saw. This is so the saw teeth cut as they enter the finish side, not when they exit it, because a blade that cuts while exiting on the finish side will often splinter the face layer.

Other tools you will need include a sharp pencil, measuring tape, a small prybar to lift the panels into place when used as a fulcrum at the floor, a small plane, a hammer, a rubber mallet (for adhesive application) and a padded 2 × 4 block, a nailset, color-coded nails, a level, a caulking gun, and tubes of panel adhesive.

Installation tips include the use of scribing to fit paneling against paneling at corners (see photo), against the ceiling, or against any irregular edge, such as a brick or stone fireplace or chimney. Scribing is done by positioning the panel within an inch of the edge to be matched. Spread the legs of the compass so they reach from the edge to be matched to the cut edge of the new panel. Place the sharp metal point of one leg of the compass against the irregular edge, and place the pencil leg of the compass on the cut line of the new panel. Now draw the compass along so the sharp metal point

follows the irregular edge, and thus moves the pencil leg of the compass so it records the irregular profile on the line to be cut. Use a saber saw to make this irregular cut, following the scribe line with precision. The scribed edge of the new panel will fit perfectly against the edge you are trying to match.

Use color-coded nails or panel adhesives to secure the paneling to the wall. If you use nails, try to position the nails so they will be concealed by the pattern of the panels: i.e., drive the nails so they are concealed in a knot or wood grain in the wood panel, or in a line or other mark on patterned paneling. The preferred method is to use panel adhesives with just enough nails to hold the panels until the adhesive sets, for a nail-and-blemish-free job.

Begin panel installation at each corner of the room by establishing a plumb line within 4 feet (the panel width) of the corner. This step, being sure to start each wall with a plumb panel, will guarantee that all panels fit on that wall will be plumb, using the first panel edge as a guide. Keep in mind that you can plumb the line with a chalkline and plumb bob, or you can use a carpenter's level to do the job. You may have to scribe the edge of the first panel, or scribe the top edge of the panel to the ceiling, to align the panel so it is plumb.

Another common mistake with paneling is miscutting openings for ducts or electrical outlets. You must measure from the ceiling down, not from the floor up, to accurately cut these openings. (You must also measure from the top down to cut openings in wallboard, not up from the floor.) Remember that the measurement must reflect the position of the installed panel: you will lift the panel up, to match the ceiling, so the measurement must be from the top down. If you measure from the floor up, then lift the panel, the opening obviously will be at the wrong height from the floor, and the outlet won't fit the hole. Slight miscuts in finished materials such as paneling can be covered up by buying oversize outlet covers, made for people like

Use carpenter's scribing technique to match paneling to uneven corners or materials such as brick or stone fireplaces. Set panel at corner, leaving slight (1") space between panels. Plumb the panel you are fitting and temporarily tack it in place. Use carpenter's dividers or compass to scribe a mark along crooked edge. Position steel point of one leg against crooked or uneven corner. Place the pencil leg on the material to be marked. Move the compass slowly along the edge, and the pencil will record uneven edge as the steel leg follows it. Use a saber saw with a fine blade to cut along scribe mark. Photo courtesy of Plywood Paneling Council.

Use a saber saw and fine blade to cut openings such as electrical outlets. Pre-drill starter holes at the corners of the marked cutout, or use a plunge cut with the saw blade. Cut along marks. Wear eye goggles when cutting. Photo courtesy of Plywood Paneling Council.

Cut out window or door openings with a circular or hand saw. To avoid overcuts at corners when using circular saw, saw to 1" from corner, then finish the cut with a handsaw. For panels less than 3/16" thick, cut with a straightedge and sharp razor knife. Photo courtesy of Plywood Paneling Council.

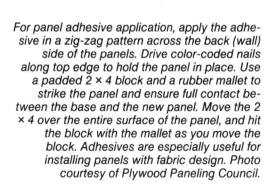

For panel adhesive application, apply the adhesive in a zig-zag pattern across the back (wall) side of the panels. Drive color-coded nails along top edge to hold the panel in place. Use a padded 2 × 4 block and a rubber mallet to strike the panel and ensure full contact between the base and the new panel. Move the 2 × 4 over the entire surface of the panel, and hit the block with the mallet as you move the block. Adhesives are especially useful for installing panels with fabric design. Photo courtesy of Plywood Paneling Council.

Turn electrical supply off while working with paneling or outlet covers. Set receptacles so ears at top and bottom rest on the face of the panels, to ensure against crooked or recessed receptacles. Note wainscot effect of wood-grain panels 32″ up from floor, fabric pattern design panels above wainscot to ceiling. Photo courtesy of Plywood Paneling Council.

Completed room. Note the cap molding (chair rail) between the wainscoting and the top panels. Note also corner molding between wall panels and ceilings. Although molding is considered a decorative plus by many people, you can eliminate the molding work and look by scribing the panels for a perfect fit at all corners. Install corner protectors to protect outside corners. Photo courtesy of Plywood Paneling Council.

us who make errors. But wide misses in cutting ruin the panel(s), so in applying finish materials the old carpenter's adage to "measure twice, cut once" is very appropriate. If you miscut a panel and ruin it for its original location, look around. You may be able to salvage your mistake by cutting it into smaller pieces to fit in headers above doors or windows, or for finishing soffits (drop ceilings).

You can fudge the joints when installing wall paneling with adhesives over wallboard, because the adhesives will hold the panel edges. When using panel adhesives, you should make a zig-zag pattern on the back of the panel. Be careful to keep your hands and tools out of the adhesive during installation, to avoid getting adhesives on the finish face of the panel.

On the other hand, you cannot fudge, or let the joints fall where they may, if you are nailing the panels on. Then you must be sure that each edge falls directly on a stud, because you must secure the edge by driving nails. It is crucial during the framing process that you keep stud spacing exactly on 16" or 24" centers, so paneling or wallboard will fit the framing without being cut for width. All wall materials are modular, made in 4' widths and in 8' or 12' lengths, so they fit without cutting on framing that is 16" or 24" on center.

As you lay out your wall panels, mark each location where a joint will occur. Select a stain that matches your panels — not the dark stain so often recommended, because your panels may not be dark — and paint a 2"-wide stripe down the backer board over each joint location. Let this stain dry (only minutes) so it does not stain hands or panels as you work, then apply the paneling so the joints fit loosely together. Wood panels may shrink slightly, or have an open joint between them: any wallboard or backer board that peeks through between the panels will not be visible if they are the same color as the paneling.

PREFINISHED GYPSUM WALL PANELS

Major wallboard manufacturers offer ½"-thick gypsum panels in 4' × 8' size, with a variety of decorative vinyl coverings. These prefinished gypsum panels are available with wood grain, print, or textured print finishes. They can be applied using color-coded nails, special panel adhesives, or a combination of nails and adhesives. The panels go up quickly, require no further finishing, and are durable and washable. The panels are available with such options as color-coded battens (to cover the joints), matching inside and outside corners, end caps, and panel divider strips. To explore this possibility, check with a local wallboard supplier. Look in your Yellow Pages under "Dry Wall Contractors Equipment & Supplies" for a dealer.

CEILINGS: TILE OR SUSPENDED PANELS

TOOL LIST
Installing Suspended Ceilings

- ☐ Chalk line
- ☐ Level
- ☐ Pencil
- ☐ Ladder
- ☐ Hammer
- ☐ Nails
- ☐ Support wires
- ☐ Pliers, wire cutting
- ☐ Measuring tape
- ☐ Razor knife
- ☐ Combination square
- ☐ Saber saw, fine blades
- ☐ Tin snips
- ☐ Eye goggles

Acoustic ceiling tile, available in 1' × 1' squares, offers improved acoustics plus easy installation. With acoustic tiles you install the ceiling first, then

Shown are two areas where you can use Duraform Gypsum Wall Panels. The gypsum panels have a plaster core like wallboard, but are covered with predecorated print or woodgrain designs. The panels can be an option for basement, garage, attic, or utility rooms, and eliminate the time and expense of wallboard taping, finishing, and painting. Photos courtesy of Gold Bond Building Products.

butt the wall panels up against the ceiling. The tile can be applied with adhesives over a wallboard base, or can be stapled to furring strips that have been nailed to the joists, 12″ o.c. the instructions for installing ceiling tiles are quite clear, as they come from the manufacturer. The only warning would be to start at the center of the room, so any partial tiles will result in even margins around the room perimeter. And, wash your hands frequently and use talcum powder to keep hands clean and dry while you are handling the (usually) white tile.

Suspended ceilings are a good option not only to let you "nail the paint on" but also to avoid much work furring and framing around multiple ceiling obstructions. Suspended ceilings not only go up quickly, they also permit access for future repairs to plumbing, heating, or electrical lines. The 2′ × 2′ or 2′ × 4′ panels can easily be lifted out of the metal grid frame that suspends them.

A major decorator's objection in the past was that the grid system lacked decorating appeal. Today, manufacturers such as Armstrong and United States Gypsum have color-coordinated the metal grids so they match the decorative panels. The panels are made of mineral fiber and are washable, fire-retardant, and add acoustic value.

Like most products aimed at the do-it-yourselfer market, suspended ceiling systems come complete with installation instructions from the manufacturer. One tip includes the advice given for acoustic tile: keep your hands clean and dry with talcum powder when you are cutting or handling the panels.

Check your ceiling and find the lowest spot, under pipes or wires. To maintain adequate headroom, you still may wish to build soffits around really low obstructions, such as low-hung furnace ducts, and install paneling, or wallboard, over the soffits.

When you have established the lowest obstacle, that point will be your ceiling height. With walls — paneling or wallboard — in place and finished,

mark the walls at the desired ceiling height and install support moldings (supplied with the ceiling material) at the ceiling height, around the entire perimeter of the room. Next, attach hanger wires to the joists at the intervals suggested in your instruction sheet. Install the main runners of the metal grid and level them with the hanger wires. The key at this point is to check level frequently, so you don't twist some wires shorter than others and thus make the main grids hang unevenly rather than level. Now snap the grid's cross tees into place, between the main runners. The final and finishing step is to lay the ceiling panels into the grid formed by the main runners and cross tees. For access to the original ceiling, or to the open framing above, just lift up and remove the panels.

One additional benefit of installing a suspended ceiling: you can install recessed fluorescent lights above the ceiling, install the suspended ceiling below the lights, then install translucent plastic panels rather than the usual acoustic ceiling panels below the fluorescent fixture(s). This recessed lighting makes excellent sense if you wish overhead (ceiling) lighting, but have limited headroom for hanging regular ceiling light fixtures. Keep in mind that the fluorescent lights are cool, and do not pose a fire hazard by generating heat as recessed incandescent lights do. (If you install recessed incandescent lighting, you must take steps to prevent excessive heat buildup. Oversized light bulbs, for example, emit more heat and thus provide more fire hazard than small light bulbs. You therefore must not exceed the recommended bulb size when installing or replacing light bulbs in these fixtures.)

FLOORCOVERING

A wide array of do-it-yourself floorcovering products is available to the consumer. Advances in adhesive technology let you lay the floor today and dance on it tonight. I urge you to seal any concrete floor before installing floor covering, especially

First, measure the maximum height you can install the ceiling, allowing for hanging obstacles. Nail the wall molding from the ceiling kit to the wall at that maximum allowable height (or desired height).
Photo courtesy of Armstrong Industries, Inc.

Install the main runners so they rest on the wall molding, and fasten them in place with hanger wires. Check your work frequently with a carpenter's level to be sure all wires are tied at same height.
Photo courtesy of Armstrong World Industries, Inc.

With the main runners in place, install the cross tees between the runners. Tabs on the tees engage the slots on the main runners, lock them in place. Photo courtesy of Armstrong World Industries, Inc.

When the metal grids are in place, drop the acoustic panels into the openings, so panel edges rest on grid flanges. The panels can be easily removed for access to plumbing or electrical work above. Photo courtesy of Armstrong World Industries, Inc.

covering that has a self-stick adhesive on the back.

Vinyl floor tiles that are peel-and-stick come in a rainbow of color options, plus patterns of stone, brick, or wood parquet. Also, there are a variety of patterns available: you can even lay out a shuffleboard pattern on the recreation room floor, using vinyl tile to make the pattern. Choose a quality tile that has a no-wax finish so they will not only be easy to install, but will require little maintenance.

In addition to vinyl floor tile, there are carpet tiles that are easy to install without the stretchers and tools required for laying ordinary carpet. Carpet tile is a common choice in office and commercial buildings, and the tiles can be pulled up and replaced if they become stained or if a wear pattern begins to show, from traffic. You may have to look for this commercial-grade carpet tile at dealers who cater to commercial/industrial accounts, or ask your local store to order the carpet tile for you. Any supplier can special-order materials, if they are only helpful enough to do so.

You can also choose to install foam or Kanga-backed carpet yourself. The foam backing adds shockproof padding underneath, but you need not go through the work of installing both a carpet and a pad, because the pad is built-in. It is helpful to lay rubber-backed carpet loose, untrimmed, with the edges folded up the wall. Let the carpet relax, or lose its wrinkles, before you try to lay it. Once it has flattened out, you can trim one edge to fit, and coat a border at the cut edge with latex carpet adhesive. An alternative is to place two two-faced carpet tape on the floor, under the edge of the carpet, then press the carpet firmly into contact with the adhesive tape.

Remember, you can rent almost any tool for any trade at your local rental dealer. Floor stretchers for carpet are among the rental items available, so if you prefer to try installing carpet hook-strip, padding, then stretching carpet over it, the tools are available.

STAIRS

For stair safety, most experts recommend that you do not carpet stair treads. The thickness of carpet and padding will reduce the usable width of the tread; using a thick padding on stairs will not only take up part of the tread width, but will also provide a surface that may hook the heel of a shoe, particularly if those shoes have ladies' spike heels.

Instead of using carpet on stairs, consider using paint, urethane floor finish, non-slip vinyl treads, or a non-slip commercial coating made for safety on stairs. Non-slip coatings are available at janitors' supply stores.

If nothing but carpet will do for your stairs, choose a tightly-woven material that has a loop finish. Install the carpet without a pad, choosing instead to replace the carpet frequently rather than to risk a trip and fall with heavy padding. Unpadded carpet will wear more quickly, because any pad would help absorb the shock of falling footprints.

Another alternative, which we discussed in Chapter 10, PAINTING, is using a quality paint on the concrete floor. This can be a practical alternative for a laundry, shop, utility, or furnace room. Just follow the directions given for floor painting.

If you choose to leave the concrete floor bare in utility areas, at least apply a sealer to make the floor easy to clean and to prevent dusting of the surface of the concrete floor. A good source of a clear, heavy-duty sealer is a janitor's store. Look for these stores in your Yellow Pages under "Janitorial Equipment & Supplies," or ask your school or church janitor to recommend a good sealer for your concrete floors.

12
Tips for Finishing Attics

The how-to advice for finishing basements works equally well for finishing any other space. Construction job procedures are the same whatever space you're finishing, so we hope you find the material useful for any project.

Attic or expansion space, however, presents a set of special problems. Some houses, usually called "Cape Cod" in design, were built with the attic space set up to be used for future expansion. These houses have steep roofs, to increase headroom; and they have heavier joists, either 2 × 8 or 2 × 10s, depending on the span, that will serve for floor joists. Most houses have 2 × 6 ceiling joists, which are large enough to support the ceiling and insulation blanket, but will not serve as floor joists.

Another problem is that finishing the attic space radically alters the insulation/ventilation requirements that served the old house design. A new system must be established to avoid future problems that will be very expensive to correct.

Most attic problems we have discussed require a contractor's expertise, because we are dealing with problems that require changes in the support structure of the house.

HEADROOM

The first problem is overhead space, or headroom. Because of the slope of most roofs, attic headroom is limited. In the Cape Cod design there is a steep roof that may slope quickly to a knee (short or partial) wall at one or both sides, but there is adequate headroom down the middle, and for a few feet on either side, to allow one to stand comfortably. If your attic does not have enough headroom you must raise the roof.

The way to raise the roof is to build a dormer. If you imagine your roof to be hinged at the ridge line, and you raised it a few feet on the outside or eave edge, you'd have a dormer. Often, that's just about what a contractor will do: in fact, some builders carefully cut out the portion of the roof that should be raised, leaving the roof and shingles intact. Then they simply jack up the outside edge of the roof, and build walls under the outside perimeter. If you don't have experience dealing with structural loading, it's best to leave dormer construction to a contractor. For example, you must double up the rafters on each side of the dormer cutout for increased roof support on both ends of the dormer.

FLOOR JOISTS

If the ceiling joists of your house were intended to be just that, to support the ceiling only, you must reinforce the floor. Floor joists obviously must support live loading, which refers to furniture, people and floorcoverings you will have in the finished space. In some instances you can set new 2 × 8 or 2 × 10 joists alongside the existing 2 × 6 ceiling joists to beef up the floor, but this step will again reduce the available headroom by either 2″ or 4″. Again, this is usually a job for a contractor. The contractor must not only install floor joists to replace the ceiling joists, he must be very careful to avoid damaging the finished ceilings in the main floor below. If you start nailing double joists into the attic, you can imagine what the pounding and vibration could do to a plaster ceiling. The contractor will not only consider what this rise in the floor level will do to the available headroom, and adjust the headroom clearance accordingly, he knows ways to raise the floor without disturbing the ceiling below, because he can extend the bearing walls with spacers and engineer the new floor to "float" above the old ceiling joists, so that the new load is not carried on the old ceiling structure.

INSULATION AND VENTILATION

With the existing house, the insulation blanket lies atop the ceilings, between or between/covering the ceiling joists. The underside of the roof deck is bare (because you never install insulation between two cold areas, only between a cold and a warm area). The roof has a series of ventilators of one or another type, and outside air can enter into the open attic space, move across the insulation blanket, pick up migrant moisture from the insulation or attic space, and carry the moisture outside, keeping the framing and insulation dry and problem-free.

When you finish the attic you must install a new insulation barrier on the underside of the roof deck, because you now want to establish the new heat loss barrier above the new living space. You can leave the old insulation in place between the joists, because it is a mess to remove it. Aside from providing some sound loss reduction between the attic and floor below, the old insulation now will serve no purpose, because you have no interest in stopping heat flow between two occupied floors or spaces.

The problem now is that you must install a new insulating barrier between the roof rafters. Often, or usually, the old rafters are 2 × 4s, which are only 3½″ thick. The problems this presents are two. First, that thickness — 3½″, the thickness or depth of a 2 × 4 — is not enough space for installing adequate insulation. A 3½″-thick insulation batt only provides 11-R, which is not enough insulation for most homes. But, you must never fill ceiling or roof cavities completely full of insulation. While a vapor barrier is advised to help prevent moisture passage into the cavity between rafters, some moisture will invariably pass through. You must leave a minimum of 1″ of free air space above the insulation, and then provide ventilation for that air space. Especially in the northern half of the country, where severe cold will turn that roof moisture to frost, you must provide for that moisture to pass out.

The solution is to extend the depth of the 2 × 4 rafters. I have nailed 2 × 2s to the bottom of 2 × 4 rafters, then installed 3½″ insulation batts in the space. The added 2 × 2s permit 1½″ of airspace above the batt insulation. I then installed continuous ridge venting (the entire ridge cap is a ventilator) and continuous eave venting, so that air could flow into the space, pick up the moisture, and be exhausted out the ridge vent. This will yield the 11-R insulation value we mentioned. For more R-value, consider attaching sheets of foam board insulating panels to the underside of the extended rafters, to add another 5-R or more (depending on the thickness of the foam panel). You then must use longer wallboard screws to attach the wallboard to the rafters, which now become ceiling joists. This setup, with extended rafters permitting free ventilation under the roof deck, plus adequate insulation, will prevent the roof moisture buildup that shows up as mildew or stains on interior ceilings, and curled shingles or rotted rafters or sheathing on the roof.

An alternative, and the preferred alternative in areas where more insulation is needed, is to demolish the old roof deck in the dormer area, build a new roof structure, and use 2 × 10 or deeper joists to achieve the higher insulation values that are recommended for your area.

TRUSS ROOFS

Throughout our conversation on finishing attic space, our thrust has been toward true attic construction, not for houses that have roof trusses. You can expand upwards, even if your roof is truss construction. But, a truss system works like Ezekiel's dry bones, with "the thigh bone connected to the hip bone," and you must not disturb or remove any portion of a roof truss without consulting with an engineer or contractor. For truss roof construction, upward expansion becomes a job for pros only.

MECHANICAL INSTALLATION

A final consideration for finishing attics is the difficulty of routing electrical wiring and plumbing lines to the new space. Every possible route is covered by plaster or wallboard, and existing mechanical service such as wires, pipes, and ducts are barriers to installing new service.

Unless your attic space is roughed in, and needs finishing only, I advise a workable compromise. Hire a contractor to build a dormer, engineer a new roof deck insulation/ventilation package, and beef up ceiling joists to floor joist standards. Once the job is roughed in, you can take over and finish the space yourself.

13
How to Hire a Contractor

Having worked in the building trades, I tend to resent any suggestion that construction people are not to be trusted. I have found no more dishonesty in the construction business than in medicine or auto repair or insurance or government. I know there are thousands of people out there who are honest as you and I, who need and appreciate your business, and who live in your community, are trying to make a life and support a family, and who are, in short, your neighbors. And, when I read about the construction scam, I always wonder "where did the author find these people?"

You don't have to do business with the guy who has an old pickup truck and out-of-state license plates, who may have left the last town one hour ahead of a posse. Surely, you wouldn't open an account and hand a cash deposit to a "banker" who stopped by your house because he "just happened to be in the neighborhood." Use the same amount of discretion when you are spending your home repair and remodeling dollars: that's your money, too. Do business with established businesspeople in your community, and avoid the something-for-nothing crowd. The key is not, as some advice columns suggest, to outwit the crook. The key is to avoid and not hire the crook, because the dishonest op-

erator will, if you invite him to dine, eat your lunch. You can take that to the bank.

The first step, if you are seeking construction help or advice, is to go to trustworthy people. One source of reputable contractors is the membership list of the National Association of Home Builders (NAHB). These are established business men and women in your community. Most NAHB members will note their membership in their advertising. Or, check with the local branch of the National Association of the Remodeling Industry (NARI). People who belong to these organizations are people who are concerned about their industry, who have a code of ethics, and who try to police their own industry.

Another source for weeding out contractors might be your local building center. If you are in the business, you quickly learn that giving someone a reference can be the source of nothing but headaches. If your friend is unhappy with the person you recommend, he or she will blame you for the problem(s). No one needs the grief of being blamed for a bad reference, so most people in the business are cautious about whom they recommend. If your building center operator will stick his neck out and recommend a contractor to you, you can generally be assured this contractor has a good track record. This is true also of your banker, your savings and loan or other credit source.

The safe path is first to choose a group of reputable people to bid, *then* ask for bids from several bidders. Be sure that the bid you get includes *in writing,* all specifications down to the finest detail, including such things as brands of materials, so you know every bidder is bidding on the same project, not an apples vs. oranges situation.

Even in situations where all bidders are honest, you must have everything in writing. Written bids are made because honest misunderstandings can arise if there is not a clear agreement spelled out. Lawyers live in fine houses because too many people try working from memory, and "I thought you said . . ." leads to litigation. Get it in writing.

In the beginning of this book I talked of the importance of good planning, of not going off on tangents. This is doubly important if you are hiring work done. Any change, no matter how small, may void your contract. In the contractor's defense, the change that seems small to you can be expensive in the execution. Finalize your plan before you make a contract, and try very hard to stick with the original script. If a change cannot be avoided, put it in writing, get a bid of the cost, and then have the contractor sign a change order with you. The cry at payoff: "But I thought you were going to throw that in" is translated by the contractor as "I changed my mind but I want you to pay," and the contractor will rightly resent it.

LIEN WAIVERS

Contractors often supply materials in addition to their services. They may also hire subcontractors, who in turn may furnish *their* own materials. The result is that many businessmen become involved financially in a job contract that was only signed by you and the prime contractor. This multiple involvement of people and money, beyond the original players, can lead to mass confusion. For example, a contractor may have been paid by you for a job. He, the contractor, paid the plumber, a subcontractor, for his job. Unfortunately, the plumber did not pay the supplier for the plumbing fixtures and appliances that he installed in your house. The cost of these fixtures can add up to thousands of dollars. Because the fixtures and appliances were installed in your house, the supplier may try to recover his bill from you. "But that's not fair!" you protest. Well, as a lawyer once said to me: "Fair? You mean the one in August, with the Ferris wheel? Where are your lien waivers?"

If we have a contract, and I owe you money, you know it, and I know it. If you file a lien against my property, the debt becomes public knowledge. A lien is public announcement that a person, or company, may have a financial interest in the ownership of a piece of property. In most instances, unless the interest is settled (the owner pays off the lien) the property can legally be sold to satisfy (pay) the lienholder.

So, get the lien waivers from not only the contractor, but also from any subcontractors who worked on the project, whether you pay the subcontractor yourself, or he is paid by the contractor as part of the overall agreement.

Financial and mortgage institutions will often be able to supply lien waivers (and may insist on having them if they granted you a home improvement loan). How important is the lien waiver? The importance increases with the amount of money involved. For example, I am a painting contractor and I did a job for you, for which I was paid $1,000. I furnished ten gallons of paint, worth perhaps $200, to do the job. I signed a lien waiver, for the total amount, or $1,000. Should you insist on having the waiver signed by the material supplier who sold me the paint? If I do not pay the supplier, he can come back at you for only the value of his paint, or $200. So your exposure is small. But, if

I am a heating subcontractor, and my bill on the job included $3,000 worth of furnace and air conditioning equipment, your exposure is much greater: $3,000 is a lot of money to most of us. So, you should insist that, in addition to the heating subcontractor signing the lien waiver, he must also get a signature from his supplier, stating that the supplier has been paid for the $3,000 worth of equipment. This ensures that the supplier cannot put a lien on your property to recover any unpaid material charges. Masonry, plumbing, and heating contractors are examples of contractors whose materials bills may be a large portion of the bid, so it is common to ask these contractors for paid material receipts or signed lien waivers from their material suppliers.

CRISIS-OF-THE-MONTH CLUB

One point that is seldom made is that there is a difference between contractors and the con men who move in and out of the construction business with enough frequency to give the industry a black eye. All legitimate contractors would like to help banish these people from the business. The opportunists who try to make a fast buck from the latest fad crisis are no more part of the construction business than Willie Sutton, bank robber, was a financier because he made his living off of banking.

The "crisis-of-the-month" club is composed of con men, alarmists, and media people who proclaim that henny penny was right, and the sky *is* going to fall, unless you spend big money to eliminate the radon, or asbestos, or whatever from your home. In the mid-1970s I saw several jobs where urea foam insulation was blown into the walls of older homes. Because of some errors in one job I had to take one of those insulated walls apart. What I saw was half-filled wall cavities, foam that had turned to powder, degraded by the sunlight which fell on the wall's exterior, header cavities (the cavities between the short studs over doors and windows) that never were touched at all. To say that I was

definitely underwhelmed by this new insulation is to put it mildly. I drew the only possible conclusion: these guys were the Jesse James' of the '70s. The damage to the exterior siding alone was enough to make anyone conclude that installing the stuff would damage your house far beyond anything it could save you in heat conservation. In addition, urea formaldehyde insulation was more than 90% water as sprayed into the wall cavities, and this hand's experience was that one *never* introduces that much water into wall cavities, where vapor barriers on the inside and building paper on the outside would prevent it from rapid escape.

The stuff was a disaster. Thousands of families paid to have that material blown into their walls, with no payback on the investment in energy savings. Far from saving energy: Chevron's study showed that energy bills actually *rose* for two years, while your furnace tried to drive all that moisture out of your walls. Who warned the public? Who tested those claims? Nobody. Certainly not the media, who were busy trying to help sell the stuff to an unsuspecting public. And, not the government, who were busy urging us all to do our bit to conserve energy. In 1990 I can show you dozens of houses in my own city where the exterior appearance was devastated by the holes bored in the siding. And, much later, urea formaldehyde was declared a health risk. So much for the crisis-of-the-month.

Today, there is a new crisis. It may be formaldehyde, or radon, or asbestos. And some of these problems may be legitimate areas of concern. I breathed asbestos fibers daily for more than twenty years, because it was part of materials I handled — and installed in your house. With today's evidence of problems for workers with long-term exposure to asbestos, I would much rather that I had never worked with the stuff. The problem can be that we cannot consider that one-time or casual exposure to the homeowner is all that great a health hazard. Listen to the Environmental Protection Agency: "Asbestos is only dangerous when its tiny fibers can be released into the air and inhaled. If the material is solid and maintained in good condition, it presents no problem." ("Asbestos in the Home," p. 18.)

The answer, I believe, is prudence. I want no further contact with asbestos, but I would not pay hundreds or thousands of dollars to have it removed from my home. I cannot believe that it requires that high level of concern.

Another crisis product is radon. It has been beaten to death by the media, and the heightened concern of the public makes us all targets for the unscrupulous dealers who make their living from the worry that these crises generate.

Do we dismiss the problems altogether? No. In Chapter 1 the reader is cautioned to test for radon; contact the EPA if there is asbestos insulation in the basement that will be disturbed by remodeling activity. What I am urging is a prudent concern, without the panic that has made thousands of families the victims of rip-offs.

Many of the so-called construction rip-offs are done by those who bounce into the latest crisis concern. They have no past references because yesterday no one knew there was a problem, as is the case with radon and asbestos. They are not really contractors, they are thieves who prey on homeowners' legitimate concerns.

The problem, as the World Champion Poker Players once observed, is that one cannot assume that all trappers wear fur hats. Some trappers wear hard hats, and some sit hatless behind their desks, ready to relieve you of the burden of your savings account. The best advice is to know with whom you are dealing and, when in doubt, do nothing. Never let a person unknown to you declare that he has come to save you from some unseen emergency.

Glossary

ACOUSTICAL MATERIALS — Any building material that has the ability to reduce sound transmission or reflection. Insulation, tiles, and texture spray materials are examples.

AGGREGATE — Material such as rock or gravel mixed with water and cement to make concrete. Sand and perlite are common aggregates used in texture paints.

AIR SPACE — The cavity formed between building materials in a wall or ceiling: for example, the space between a pair of studs or rafters that is enclosed by wallboard on one side and sheathing material on the opposite side.

ANGLE IRON — L-shaped steel support used to support masonry over fireplace opening or to support a load above a window or door.

ATTIC VENTILATORS — Roof or gable openings that permit air to circulate. Ventilators may be static, as louvers, or power vents aided by a motor and fan.

BACKFILL — Excavated earth that is returned to fill the void against a basement wall, or to fill a trench, following construction activity.

BACKING — Wood or other material that is installed to provide support for finish materials: i.e., scrap wood installed at corners to provide nailers for wallboard.

BASE SHOE — Molding used to cover the crack between the base trim and floor or carpet.

BASEMENT — Lower or support floor of a building; floor that is totally or partially below grade.

BATT — Material, usually insulation, that is formed into a slab, to fit between framing members. Insulation batts may be faced on one side with a vapor barrier of kraft paper or aluminum foil.

BEAM — Horizontal support member used to carry load across a span. A beam is supported on both ends, sometimes with intermediate support posts to the floor, and in turn carries weight of floor joists above. Often wood; if beam is steel it may be called an I-beam.

BEAM CEILING — A ceiling in which the beams are exposed; they may actually support the roof load but often are added for decorative effect only.

BEARING WALL OR PARTITION — Any wall or partition that supports, or *bears,* weight from above. As opposed to a non-bearing wall or curtain wall that is a visual or weather barrier supporting no weight but its own.

BID — A proposal to perform a specified job. The bid also should include *specifications* (also called a "spec sheet") that spell out the labor, materials, and total price agreed upon.

BLIND NAILING — Nails driven so nailheads are not visible. Nails driven at an angle through the tongue of hardwood flooring, so the groove of the adjoining board conceals the nailheads, are "blind nailed."

BLOCK — In masonry, refers to a concrete building unit used for building walls. A basement wall may be laid up with mortar and concrete blocks rather than being formed and poured concrete.

BOTTOM OR SOLE PLATE — The bottom framing member of a wall, usually either 2 × 4 or 2 × 6. The plate is nailed to the bottom of the studs and to the floor joist or sheathing below it.

BRIDGING — Wood or steel braces installed in an "X" pattern or diagonally between floor joists to prevent joists from twisting and to transfer loading between joists.

BUILDING CODE — Standards set by a community to ensure safety, strength, and value of buildings.

BUNDLE — Building materials held together by nylon or steel strapping: bundles are formed for ease of handling and shipping materials and for easy calculation of contents: a bundle of shingles is 1/3 of a square, or 33 sq. ft. A square of shingles thus covers 100 sq. ft. of roof.

CARRIAGE — Framing members that support stair steps or treads.

CEMENT — Powder produced when clay and limestone are burned; when mixed with sand and/or gravel and water it makes concrete.

CENTER TO CENTER — Distance between two framing members as measured from the center of one to the center of the next; often expressed as "on center." The distance between two framing members is usually 16″ or 24″ o.c.

CERAMIC TILES — Tiles made of vitreous clay and used as a surface cover or finish on walls, floors, or ceilings.

CHALK LINE — Metal or plastic container that is tear-shaped and holds powdered chalk and a strong cord or line. When the line is pulled out, it is coated with chalk powder: held by both ends and snapped over a mark, it leaves a line that can be used as a visual or cutting guide.

CLEANOUT — A plumbing joint that is equipped with a removable cover that one can open to clean the pipe.

CLINCH — To drive a nail completely through the lumber so the tip protrudes on the backside. The tip is then bent over to increase holding power of the nail.

COMBUSTIBLE/INCOMBUSTIBLE — Terms referring to a material's ability to support combustion: incombustible refers to materials that will not support combustibles if subjected to house fire temperatures, generally between 1200° and 1700° F.

COMMON WALL — The wall that separates two or more apartments, townhouses, or condominiums.

CONCRETE — A mix, usually water/cement/sand/gravel, used for floors, foundations, or basement construction.

CONDUIT — Metal pipe used to route and protect electrical wiring.

CORNER BEAD — Sheet metal strip formed to 90°, nailed on outside corners to provide a strong, straight edge for finishing corners in wallboard construction.

CORNER STUDS — Wall studs nailed together to form a 90° inside corner, as where two walls meet.

COUNTERSINK — To sink nails, bolts, or screws so that the heads are below the surface of the workpiece.

COURSES — Building materials installed in rows or layers; for example, rows of concrete block in a basement wall are called courses.

CRIPPLE — A short framing stud that is cut off to make an opening for a door or window.

CROSS VENTILATION — Ventilation provided at opposite ends of a room or building, so that moving air can circulate through the entire length of the space. Windows open on opposite walls are said to provide cross ventilation.

CURING — A chemical reaction between water and plaster or cement, sometimes called hardening.

CURTAIN WALL — Any wall that does not support weight except its own; a non-bearing wall.

DAMP PROOF — To coat the exterior side of a concrete basement wall with cement or asphalt mix, so that moisture cannot penetrate the wall.

DEAD LOAD — The weight of all the materials in a building, added together, is called the dead load. The live load is the weight of the occupants and furnishings.

DEADENING — Materials or building techniques intended to stop noise transfer are called deadening.

DEHUMIDIFIER — An appliance designed to reduce the humidity or moisture levels in the air.

DEW POINT — Temperature at which moisture condenses. In installing insulation and vapor barriers, it is important to avoid creating multiple dew points in a wall or ceiling, where moisture might collect.

DOOR STOP — A strip on the inside or face of a door frame, that stops a door at midpoint on the frame.

DOUBLE HEADER — On bearing walls, the headers over door or window openings must support weight from above, so two header boards are nailed together for extra strength. Double headers are also necessary to support floors cut open for stair openings.

DOWNSPOUT — The plastic or metal pipe that carries roof water from the gutter to the ground pipe.

DUCT — A round or rectangular pipe, usually made of sheet metal, used to distribute cool or hot air throughout the house.

EFFLORESCENCE — White, powdery material that appears on concrete as a result of salts migrating out from inside the concrete mass.

ESTIMATE — An advance calculation of the cost of a project; may be for materials, labor, or both.

EXCAVATE — To remove earth from a basement site or utility trench, by means of a bulldozer or backhoe (a backhoe is a tractor with a scoop bucket attached).

EXIT — Means or avenue of moving from one part of a building to another part, or for leaving the building for an open space.

FALSE CEILING — A drop or suspended ceiling, hung on metal or wood grids, to permit covering exposed ducts, pipes, or beams.

FEATHER — To trowel to a thin edge, as when finishing wallboard joints.

FIRE STOP — A barrier installed to prevent drafting or spread of fire or flames; can be 2 × 4 or other studs installed horizontally between vertical studs.

FIRE WALL — A wall of proven fire resistance that is installed between two dwellings (as between townhouses) or between a house and attached garage. Required by building codes to stop fire spreading through a building.

FLIGHT — A section of stairs that joins two floors in a house, as a flight of stairs.

FLOOR DRAIN — A water drain and trap installed at a low point in the basement floor, so that any water that enters the basement can flow out through main drains into the sewer.

FLUSH — Even or straight, as a door should be installed flush to the wall.

FOOTING — The masonry (or wood in wood basements) base which supports the basement walls and the weight of the building above. The footing by code is as thick as the basement wall is thick, and twice as wide as the wall is thick. Thus, a basement built out of 12″ block would have a footing of poured concrete that is 12″ thick and 24″ wide.

FOUNDATION — The masonry or, lately, wooden structure that is installed between the building and the earth.

FRAME — The finish woodwork around a door or window opening.

FRAMING — The portion of the building that forms the support: studs, joists, and rafters are framing.

FROSTLINE — The point in the soil to which frost penetrates in freezing weather. Footings should be built below the frostline, so the earth underneath them cannot freeze and heave. This soil depth can be four feet (48″) in the northern tier of states. Check local building department for your frostline depth.

FURRING CHANNEL — The horizontal support in the grid that holds a suspended ceiling.

GRADE — The slope of the ground surface around a house, established so the lawn slopes away from the foundation.

GROUND FLOOR — the floor of a house that is at or near the finished grade.

GROUT — Mortar or other filler used to fill joints between masonry or ceramic tiles.

GUTTER — Metal or fiberglass channel that is installed at the eaves to collect rain from the roof and direct it to the ground.

GYPSUM — Optional term that refers to wallboard; more specifically the plaster core between the two layers of paper on a wallboard panel.

H-BEAM — Steel support beam placed down the middle of a basement to hold the floor joists; called an H-beam or I-beam, depending on width of top and bottom flanges.

HEAD ROOM — Vertical space between the floor and ceiling, stairs and ceiling (in a stairway), or between the floor and header on a door opening.

HEADER — Horizontal lumber support that is installed over the top of door or window openings. The header supports the weight of the roof and roof framing.

INSULATING BOARD — Panels, usually 4′ × 8′, that provide insulation value. May be fiberboard or beadboard (made of Styrofoam beads).

INSULATION — Any material that provides a barrier to passage of heat, electricity, or sound.

JAMB — Material that surrounds or cases a window or door opening. Top, horizontal piece is called the head jamb; vertical pieces at both sides are side jambs.

JOINT CEMENT — Material available in powder (to be mixed with water) or in paste form (ready-mixed) used for finishing joints in wallboard construction. Also called "mud" (by pros), taping compound, or taping cement.

JOIST — Parallel framing members, spaced 16″ or 24″ on center, that support either the floor or ceiling.

JOIST HANGER — Metal device, shaped like a "U," used to connect two joists or a joist and beam at right angles to each other.

LAG SCREW — A wood screw that has a head like a bolt, driven with a wrench rather than a screwdriver.

LAMINATE — Act of joining two workpieces together using adhesive. Alternately, the finish material known as plastic laminate used in cabinet and furniture construction.

LANDING — A platform that joins or terminates flights of stairs.

LATH — Base material for plaster of stucco; can be wood, gypsum, or steel (wire).

LEVEL — Tool used to establish horizontal or vertical (plumb) lines.

LIVE LOAD — Weight of materials that are not part of the house, as furniture and appliances; also weight (combined) of occupants of house; as opposed to "dead load," the weight of the house itself.

LOCK SET — Complete set of hardware including the lock, knobs, screws, and strike plate.

MASONRY — Term that encompasses concrete or tile materials used in construction.

MASTIC — Coating or adhesive material often used in reference to ceramic tile adhesive or vinyl adhesive for tile or sheet goods.

MATCHED JOINT — Wood joint that is closely fitted, either with glue or with tongue-and-groove joinery.

MECHANICAL EQUIPMENT — All devices installed by the "mechanical trades," i.e., electrical, heating and air conditioning, plumbing materials and equipment.

MESH — Metal wire reinforcing base for plaster or concrete.

MOISTURE BARRIER — Any material (usually building paper or polyethylene plastic sheets) used to block the flow of moisture or vapor through walls, ceilings, or floors.

NAIL POPS — Also called "fastener failure," is also common in screw application of wallboard. Caused by shrinkage of framing members after wallboard is installed. Prevention: use construction adhesives, dry lumber.

NONBEARING WALL — Wall or partition that provides a curtain or barrier to passage, but does not support any structural load.

OAKUM — Filler, usually rope material soaked in tar, used to fill joints or caulk between materials. Available at plumbing supply stores, as plumber's oakum, used to fill bell housing on drain pipes.

OFFSET — Ledge or recess where there is a change in material or wall thickness.

ON CENTER (O.C.) — The interval between framing members such as studs, joists, or rafters is always expressed as "on center," or o.c., rather than "between" to avoid confusion. The measurement refers to the distance from the center of one framing member to the center of the next framing member.

PARGING — Coat of mortar, usually cement, applied to damp-proof concrete basement walls. The material is troweled on the outside of the wall.

PARQUET — Small squares of wood applied to floor or other surface in a pattern.

PERM FACTOR — Rate at which moisture or vapor moves through a wall or ceiling and each or all of its components — framing, wallboard, vapor barrier, etc.

PERPENDICULAR — Measurement or material as seen straight up and down or plumb, as opposed to side to side or horizontal.

PIER — Base, usually concrete, that supports posts or other loads.

PLAN — Horizontal section drawing of a house that shows size, shape, location of doors, windows, walls, and equipment.

PLASTER BOARD — Optional term used to refer to wallboard, gypsum board.

PLATE, SILL — The flat framing member, usually a 2 × 6 or 2 × 8, that is bolted to the foundation and is a base for the rim joists around the perimeter of the foundation or basement wall.

POST — Timber or metal pipe placed on end to support any load above it.

PREFINISHED — Refers to building components that are delivered to the buyer with the finish already applied at the factory: flooring, cabinets, paneling.

PREHUNG DOOR — A door that is purchased as an assembled unit, already installed with hinges in a frame and pre-bored to receive the lockset.

PUTTY — Pliable filler material used to fill wood holes or to seal glass in a window; also plumber's putty, used around sink rims, etc.

QUARTER ROUND — Wood molding that describes a 90° arc, or quarter of a circle.

R VALUE — The "R" stands for "resistance" to heat flow, and is a means of measuring the value of materials used for thermal insulation.

ROCK WOOL — Insulation made from silica or other rock material.

ROUGH HARDWARE — Hardware or fasteners used in framing, such as nails, bolts, or lag screws.

ROUGHING IN — The preliminary or first stage of the work: for plumbing, for example, roughing in is the term for routing all supply and waste pipes to their locations, ready for fixture installation.

SCAB — A short piece of lumber that is placed so it bridges the joint between two pieces of lumber that are laid out with a butt joint. The scab is then fastened so it connects the two pieces of lumber.

SCRIBING — Cutting and marking wood or other material so its edge matches the surface it butts up to, as the edge of a cabinet or paneling against a wall.

SECTION — Sometimes called a "through section," an illustration that shows a structure in cross-section.

SHIM — A piece of wood, often a wood shingle with a wedge shape, placed to level or plumb cabinets, door frame, or windows.

SHOW MOLDING — A molding strip that covers the crack between the baseboard and the floor.

SLEEPER — A sort of furring strip for floors: a wood strip that is embedded in or fastened to a concrete or wood floor to provide nailers or leveling as needed.

SOFFIT — Soffits are sometimes called "drop ceilings," are the underside of eaves (exterior) or the lowered area above cabinets in the kitchen or bath.

SOIL STACK — The vertical drain pipe that provides waste flow downward and ventilation upward through the roof.

SOUND TRANSMISSION — Usually expressed in decibels as the unit of measurement; the sound that passes through a given material or building unit.

SPALLING — Deterioration of the face of a masonry wall, usually caused by moisture or frost problems.

SPAN — The distance separating supporting members such as beams or bearing walls.

SPECIFICATIONS — A detailed list that shows the size and quality or brand of materials to be used in construction.

STC — Sound Transmission Class; relates via decibel loss how resistant a building unit is to sound passage.

STRINGER — A support for joists or other framing members: in stairs, the members that support the steps or treads.

STUD — The framing members that support the walls, to which the wallboard is fastened on the inside and sheathing/siding is fastened on the outside.

SUBFLOOR — The first or primary layer of wood that covers the top of the floor joists.

SUSPENDED CEILING — A ceiling usually supported by wires and hung beneath the level of the joists. Suspended ceilings are often chosen where ducts, pipes, or framing prevent installation of a level ceiling.

TAPING — The term used in wallboard construction that refers to the entire process of finishing the wallboard, including sealing the joints with wallboard tape and applying two trowel coats that level the joints.

TEMPLATE — A full-sized pattern, often cut from builder's paper and used for layout purposes. Also, an adjustable tool used to mark hinge locations on a door edge, called a "hinge template."

TOTAL RUN — The overall horizontal measurement of a stair.

UNDERLAYMENT — Material used as a base for applying some finish material, as carpet underlayment.

VANITY — The base cabinet or counter in a bathroom.

VAPOR BARRIER — A barrier, usually aluminum foil, kraft paper, or polyethylene plastic, that is installed in the warm side of a wall, ceiling, or floor to slow moisture or vapor penetration. Also serves as a barrier to air infiltration.

WALLBOARD — Panels consisting of a plaster core and front and back covers of paper, used for interior finish in place of plaster. Often called plaster board or Sheetrock®, which is a trade name.

WORKING DRAWINGS — Detailed project drawings that provide a guide for construction.

Appendix

TELEPHONE LIST
SUPPLIERS & SUBCONTRACTORS

Supplier/Subcontractor Name	Contact	Phone	Bid Amount
Lumber Yard:			
Home Center:			
Decorating:			
Plumbing:			
Electrical:			
Heating:			
Contractor:			
Excavator:			
Plumber:			
Electrician:			
Drywall:			
Painter:			
Paperhanger:			
Bldg. Dept.:			
Inspectors:			
OTHER:			

PROJECT GUIDE

Planning

Notes

DECIDE on use of space

LAY OUT room dimensions on floor

INSPECT concrete walls for cracks

INSPECT joists and existing framing for alighment

DRAW working plan to scale

MAKE multiple copies of plan

SUBMIT plans to Building Department

SUBMIT plans for bids, estimates

MAKE supplier, contractor choices

PATCH and waterproof concrete walls, floors

FRAME walls, install backing

ROUGH-IN plumbing

ROUGH-IN electrical, phones

ROUGH-IN heating

INSTALL fireplace

CALL for first inspection

INSULATE

INSTALL vapor barrier

INSTALL wallboard, tile board

TAPE and finish wallboard

PRIME wallboard

TEXTURE ceilings

INSTALL paneling

FINISH closet interiors

INSTALL vanity, cabinets

TRIM, install doors

SET ceramic tile

PAINT, stain

INSTALL electrical devices

SET plumbing fixtures

FINISH electrical, hang lighting

HANG wallcovering

CLEAN rooms, floors

LAY carpet

CALL for final inspection

JOB SCHEDULE

Project	Materials Bought	Date Begun	Date Finished	Inspected
Framing				
Electrical, rough				
Plumbing, rough				
Heating				
Insulation				
Wallboard				
Wallboard, finishing				
Trim				
Ceramic tile				
Painting				
Wallcovering				
Suspended ceilings				
Finish lighting fixtures				
Floorcovering				
Set fixtures, plumbing				

OWNER'S INSPECTION CHECKLIST — PLUMBING

NOTES

_____ Water heater is set and hooked up.

_____ Main water shut-off valve is in place, easily accessible, and works properly.

_____ Water faucets on all water supply pipes: hot water is on the left, cold water is on the right.

_____ Check faucets at tub, vanity, laundry to be sure faucets are working and are not restricted.

_____ Check water pressure and volume flow by turning on all faucets and flushing toilet simultaneously. Only minimum drop in water flow should be noted.

_____ Run clothes washer through wash cycle. Check for leaks and water hammer noises in water supply pipes.

_____ Check tub, shower stall, toilet, and ceramic tile for any chipping or damage to the finishes.

_____ Turn all faucets on and off quickly and listen for water hammer or vibration noises in pipes.

_____ Check all drains for water flow. Run showers and tubs with faucets wide open.

_____ If you haven't already done so, have a professional clean all drains, including the main drain all the way to the sewer at the street.

_____ Run water down each branch drain and listen for bubbling or gurgling noises that indicate insufficient venting.

_____ If extra roof vents for plumbing have been installed, check the roof for proper vent flashing.

_____ In stocking feet, stand in new tubs or showers to be sure they are firmly in place and tub or shower base does not move or rock. Check also for a "kerplunk" noise in fiberglass shower base as you step into or out of the shower. Any noise indicates a poor-quality base that flexes with a person's weight: the thin base will soon crack from flexing, leaving you with an expensive problem — a leaking base.

_____ Call for final plumbing inspection. An experienced inspector may catch code violations that can be corrected before they cause you problems and added expense.

OWNER'S INSPECTION CHECKLIST — ELECTRICAL

_____ Electrical outlets per code, no more than 12 ft. apart. Switches black (power) wire only.

_____ Outlet boxes are positioned so front edge of box is flush with wallboard or paneling.

_____ Room circuits are 15 amp; laundry room circuits per equipment needs.

_____ All bath, laundry circuits have ground fault circuit interrupters for wet shock protection.

_____ All circuits are grounded. Check to be sure system grounding has not been interrupted due to plumbing or other changes.

_____ Bath ventilator fans are installed and working properly.

_____ Dimmer switches installed as per specifications.

_____ Furnace and central air are operational.

_____ No scratches or damage to new appliances: check laundry, furnace and dehumidifier.Security system, smoke alarms are installed and working.

_____ All lighting is in place, fixtures attached, switches working.

_____ Intercom, radio, phones are connected and working.

_____ Hot tubs, whirlpool baths are installed and working. CAUTION: Switches should not be within reach of the tub.

_____ Circuit tester or voltmeter shows 117 volts at outlets and fixtures. Check between ground and each socket.

_____ Central vacuum cleaner has been installed and is operational.

_____ Check recessed light fixtures for recommended bulb size. Oversize bulbs generate too much heat for recessed lighting safety. Use only recommended bulb sizes.

_____ 3 or 4-way switches are installed and work from every location.

_____ Electrical wiring that runs across unfinished (concrete) wall is enclosed in thinwall conduit for protection.

_____ Outlet covers are in place on all outlets and switches.

_____ Final inspection has been completed and signed off by inspector.

_____ Warranties on all equipment and appliances have been filed away for future reference.

NOTES

_____
_____
_____
_____
_____
_____
_____
_____
_____
_____
_____
_____
_____
_____
_____
_____
_____
_____
_____
_____
_____
_____
_____
_____
_____
_____
_____
_____
_____

OWNER'S INSPECTION CHECKLIST — DRYWALL (WALLBOARD)

NOTES

_____ Before application begins, check that all wiring, plumbing, framing are in place. Make final check of insulation and vapor barrier.

_____ Insist on premier installation techniques. All wallboard applied perpendicular to framing; 1″ wallboard screws as fasteners; wallboard adhesive used in all areas where there is no vapor barrier.

_____ Be sure no vapor barrier is added in bath areas where water resistant wallboard is used. Vapor barrier under water resistant board is prohibited by manufacturers.

_____ Water resistant board will sag if used on ceilings. Use regular wallboard for bath ceilings.

_____ All-metal, nail-on corner beads to be used on all outside corners. Glue-on corner bead can be easily damaged by impact blows.

_____ All outside corner bead, joints, nail or screw heads to receive not less than three (3) coats of taping/finishing compound. Texture paint will not flatten or "hide" joints with excess shrinkage or two coat finish.

_____ Spray texture ceilings will look better if they receive a first coat of primer. Prime coat ceilings before spraying.

_____ Check textured surfaces for uniform appearance, complete coverage. Check texture from several angles to find skips or "holidays" in texture.

_____ At night, with lights out, apply strong sidelight to walls, using trouble light with bare bulb held near wall. Look down the wall and check for hollow nail or screw heads, hollow or "starved" joints, loose or bubbled tape, rough edges. This inspection is most easily done after walls are primed.

_____ Mark any blemishes or rough spots with a pencil, so you can find them in daylight. Do not use a ballpoint pen or a marker for this step: the ink or dye bleeds through most paints, making it difficult to hide.

_____ Check inside corners to be sure they are square, not loaded with taping compound. Corners that are not square make trim application difficult.

_____ Save large scraps of wallboard for future repairs.

_____ Some drywall contractors do not cover new wallboard, but instead overspray at the corners, then scrape away the texture on the walls. Check to be sure the scraping process has left the corners smooth, without piles of texture at corners to interfere with wall decoration.

OWNER'S INSPECTION CHECKLIST — TRIM AND DOORS

Trim

NOTES

_____ All trim is in place, including base, shoe, moldings, stops.

_____ Chair rails, crown moldings in place as specified.

_____ All joints are clean-cut and tight-fitting. Miter joints are tight and well-fit, both re the wall surfaces and the adjoining trim.

_____ Fireplace mantel is installed and finished.

_____ Trim is grade specified and free of blemishes or defects.

_____ Nails are set below trim surface.

_____ All paneling and shelving is in place and finished per specifications.

_____ Stair rails, balusters, stringers are in place and well anchored. Treads are solid and squeak-free.

Doors

_____ All doors correct size, style, and type.

_____ Doors swing freely and quietly. Open doors will remain in any position without moving.

_____ Door knobs, latches, and hinges are properly set and aligned. Latches align with latch plates.

_____ Any exterior door(s) lock properly, open easily.

_____ All exterior door locks are keyed alike, to avoid dealing with multiple keys.

_____ All doors open in correct direction, i.e., right or left hand. NOTE: Stand inside room so door will open towards you. If knob is on right hand side, it's a right hand door; if knob is on left hand side, it's a left hand door. Remember: Door must open _toward_ you in this test.

_____ Doors are plumb against their jambs. Check crack around door for even fit and good alignment.

_____ Nails are set below surface of trim; no hammer dents or split wood; miter joints fit tightly.

_____ Any thresholds are installed and properly adjusted.

_____ Any exterior doors are weather stripped.

_____ Door bottom is at right height for good clearance over carpet, tile, etc.

_____ Door stops are properly set so door fits snugly against stop but latches without force.

_____ Exterior doors are fitted with deadbolt locks for security.

OWNER'S INSPECTION CHECKLIST — PAINTING

_____ All wallboard to be primed with USG First Coat or heavy-bodied latex paint. Finish coat to be quality latex of prescribed gloss level — flat, semi or high gloss.

_____ Check walls for coverage, neatness, corners neatly cut in to present a straight appearance.

_____ Insist that the painter will spackle any blemishes overlooked by drywall taper, or nicks and scratches on walls inflicted during trim and finish steps.

_____ Check all painted surfaces to be sure the paint is evenly applied: no lap marks, roller ridges, or brush marks permitted.

_____ Check trim, paneling, and cabinetry for paint spatters and runs.

_____ All trim to be at least two coats, nail holes to be puttied.

_____ Slip the foot from a pair of pantyhose over your hand, and move the covered hand over the finished wood. There should be no snags or rough spots.

_____ Check door edges, and top and bottom ends, to be sure they are sealed so moisture cannot penetrate.

_____ Check attention to detail. Check inside of cabinet doors, cabinet and closet shelves, being sure nothing has been skipped.

_____ Check hardware, ceramic tile, and countertops for paint runs and spatters. Insist they be cleaned.

_____ Leftover paint to remain for future touchup. Unused full gallons to be returned and credited to owner's account (some special color mixes cannot be returned).

_____ Check wallcoverings for pattern match, closed seams, uniformity of color and pattern.

_____ Inspect wallcovering job from oblique (angled) lighting for perspective. This will reveal any adhesive or other stains on the surface of the covering.

_____ Buy and save at least one roll of each wallcovering pattern, for future repairs. This ensures the material will not be "out of stock" if you need it in the future.

_____ Colors can be deceiving. If you find a color you've chosen does not appear true to the color chart once it's on the wall or ceiling, do not insist on immediate repainting. Live with the job for several days, checking the color in changing light conditions, because color can change dramatically with the time of day and type of lighting.

_____ Keep a diary of your job and record the brand and color of paint, the name and stock number of wallcovering, brand and color of ceramic tile, carpet, etc. Keep the book for reference and update it as you redecorate. When you sell the house, it is a welcome gift to the new owner.

NOTES

_____

_____

_____

_____

_____

_____

_____

_____

_____

_____

_____

_____

_____

_____

_____

_____

_____

_____

_____

_____

_____

_____

_____

_____

_____

_____

_____

Index